70 Reminders for Women
(Myself Included)

Paula A. Odhiambo

Unless otherwise marked, all Scripture quotations are taken from the Holy Bible, King James Version.

70 REMINDERS FOR WOMEN (MYSELF INCLUDED)
Copyright © 2019 Paula Odhiambo
Published by WriteMotive Shirel Books
Cover photo: eskipaper.com
Cover design: Paula Odhiambo
ISBN: 978-9966-132-26-0

All rights reserved. No part of this publication may be reproduced, stored in a retrieval system, or transmitted, in any form or by any means – electronic, mechanical, photocopying, recording or otherwise – without the prior written permission of the author.

Printed in the United States of America

DEDICATION

To the woman.

ACKNOWLEDGMENTS

I'm grateful to God for His grace and mercy, and for loving me enough to send His Son to die for me.

I'm grateful to God for my family – to list their contributions would require another book.
I love you all.

I'm grateful to God for every friend who encourages me, keeps me accountable, and does not hesitate to correct or rebuke me when the need arises.

I'm grateful to God for Wamuyu Big, whose words, "It's about time," prompted me to begin this project.

I'm grateful to God for anyone and everyone who contributed to this book by sharing experiences, being examples, advising, and praying for and with me.

I take nothing for granted.

Dear Woman,

Thank you for reading this book. My prayer is that God will use it to bless you. Please read it with a Bible by your side and verify every statement with the Word of God. I recommend this approach for any book you read.

I like to share a tip with women, a simple strategy to help them get through things like this book with as little drama and frustration as possible.

This simple tip is one I am challenged to continue implementing, and makes up the first reminder:

1

Stop, Drop and Roll

STOP trying to justify sin.
DROP the phoniness, compromise, and idols.
ROLL with what the Word of God says.

AS I READ THIS BOOK, MY PRAYER IS:

_____
_____
_____
_____
_____
_____
_____
_____
_____
_____
_____
_____
_____
_____
_____
_____

2

Show me your friends, and I will show you your future.

When God showed me this truth, I was not aware how profoundly it would impact people – myself included. I am grateful to Him each time I hear a woman say it, because it means that it is finally sinking in.

It can be a difficult truth to face, but the truth is that those we allow around us often influence the paths we take in life. David said, in Psalm 1:

> *Blessed is the man*
> *That walketh not in the counsel of the ungodly,*
> *Nor standeth in the way of sinners,*
> *Nor sitteth in the seat of the scornful.*

Notice the progression, which was described once in a women's meeting I attended. Here's a picture. Jane is heading to work. When she gets to her bus stop, she is informed that *matatus* are on strike and she will have to make the long trek to the city centre. Alarmed, and yet relieved that she left the house early, she quickly reaches into her handbag, takes off a pair of flats and throws them onto the ground, and then takes off her heels and quickly wears her flats and throws the heels into her bag.

"I understand the struggle," a female voice says. She turns. Another woman is lacing her rubber shoes. They both laugh.

"I'm Sylvia," the lady says, and stretches out her hand. Jane is aware of the dangers of reciprocating, given the stories she has heard in the news about people shaking hands with strangers and then getting robbed. But this time, she shakes a stranger's hand.

"Which way are you going?" Sylvia asks.

Their offices are not too far from each other, and so they begin the long trek. They find out that they have many life experiences in common. Jane agrees to make a short detour in order to escort Sylvia to her building. After what seems like a short time, they find themselves at the entrance of Sylvia's office building. The conversation is so enthralling that they stand at the doorway for about half an hour. Finally, after security tells them to get out of the way, they find an outdoor bench to sit on.

*

"Be not deceived," Paul says. "Evil communications corrupt good manners." To put it in today's language: "Bad company corrupts good morals."

Why does he begin by saying "Do not be deceived?"

Perhaps because this, like other verses that begin the same way, speaks about an area of life that many women take for granted.

"But Jesus hung out with prostitutes and tax collectors and was even accused of being a drunkard!"

Fair enough. Are you Jesus? What are the odds, in this world, that you will involve yourself, consistently, in evil activities, and not be tainted? What does it do to your witness when, even if you do not partake of evil activities, you are constantly seen with those who do? Can a woman leave her boyfriend's house at 8am and not be seen as having fornicated with him, even if she hasn't? And even if she hasn't, can her boyfriend then go and caution his neighbor against fornication, or encourage another neighbor to be a good example to others?

The Bible says that he who walks with the wise will become wise, but a companion of fools will be destroyed (Proverbs 13:20). Not foolish, but destroyed. That implies that regardless of a person's level of spiritual growth, intellect, even wisdom, the company around the person can destroy him or her. Be intentional about keeping godly people around you, especially women.

God, as I reflect on my friendships, these are the needs I present to You:

_____
_____
_____
_____
_____
_____
_____
_____
_____
_____
_____
_____
_____
_____
_____

3
Do you want a husband, or do you want to be a wife?

This is another question I am grateful has become fairly commonplace – so much so, in fact, that it has been asked back to me at least twice. Glory to God. There is a difference between having a husband and being a wife. A wife always has a husband, but not all women who have husbands are wives.

Look at this question carefully. How you answer will determine how you choose to pray, the state of your marital life and the temperature of your marriage.

What does it mean to be a wife?

4

A woman's arrow can never miss its target.

This proverb of the Luo people of Kenya wowed me from the very day I read it.

Every woman must gather the wisdom that helps her to understand how to harness that power God put in her to be an influencer. While on the one hand we have Rahab, and Esther, and the Shunammite, and Bathsheba, and so many others, we also have Delilah, who succeeded in acquiring information that the Philistines – a king and his army of men - failed to get several times; Jezebel, who so influenced her husband that the Bible records that there was no man who did more to provoke the Lord to anger than Ahab did; the women of Proverbs 2 and 6 and 7; etc. There is enough power in just one woman to finish an entire army.

Women have used their influence to split churches and families. What if we used this God-given power for good?

This Luo proverb once brought to my mind the verses in 2 Samuel 6:

David returned to bless his household. And Michal the daughter of Saul came out to meet David, and said, How glorious was the king of Israel today, who uncovered himself today in the eyes of the handmaids of his servants, as one of the base fellows shamelessly uncovers himself! And David said unto Michal, It was before the LORD, who chose me before your father, and before all his house, to appoint me ruler over the people of the LORD, over Israel: therefore will I make merry before the LORD. And I will yet be more contemptible than this, and will be abased in my own sight: and of the maidservants whom you have spoken, of them shall I be held in honor. Therefore Michal the daughter of Saul had no child unto the day of her death.

Did you see that? *Therefore Michal...had no child unto the day of her death.**

"Therefore", meaning the reason for her having no child is the fact that she despised her husband and his unashamed praise. This, I knew. However, one day, I asked myself, *Why was the fact that she despised her husband so abominable that she ended up being reproached herself with the kind of situation that was looked down on in her generation?*

Could it be because of a woman's power of influence? Could it have been that her words could so sting the king of Israel that he might be derailed from his cause?

I want to suggest that perhaps the Lord knew just how powerful her words were that He humbled her instantly for her husband's sake.

A woman's arrow can never miss its target.

> Be confident.
> Aim wisely.
> Shoot masterfully.

If your fellow woman aims harmfully at you, take it to the Lord in prayer, and "agree with your adversary quickly" (Matthew 5:25).

(*Michal's other children were from a previous marriage.)

Forgive me, God, for:

_____
_____
_____
_____
_____
_____
_____
_____
_____
_____
_____
_____
_____
_____

5

Perfectionism in an imperfect world is a sure ticket to misery.

There are two things we often mix up: perfection and excellence. Perfectionism is defined by the dictionary as "a personal standard, attitude or philosophy that demands perfection and rejects anything less," or "a refusal to accept any standard short of perfection."

When it comes to human beings, perfection is flawlessness and faultlessness. Excellence, on the other hand, is "the best".

In a fallen world, perfection is impossible. People sin, they have different personalities, they have different standards and different appearances. However, excellence, the art of giving one's best, is possible because if a person does things excellently, it does not mean these things will not have flaws. There may be errors — even failures — but those will not mean that the best was not attempted.

Perfection is largely about the exterior, but excellence is from the heart. If, while walking down the street, God tells you to smile at a stranger and you feel that it is beneath you, yet you continue your stroll down the street to lead a crusade where 3000 people are born again, have you done excellently?

It is wise to avoid expecting perfection from others, or to use the human gauge of perfection to judge our own efforts.

Remember, Excellent is God's Name (Psalm 8, Psalm 36:7) and He alone is perfect. Keeping this in mind will help us extend grace to others.

6

If you constantly fault-find, you'll consistently find fault.
(She who delights in fault-finding will doubtless find fault.)

When it comes to fault-finding, I can assure you this: "seek and you shall find."

Fault-finding is different from discerning, and even discernment, like Corrie ten Boom said, is a call to prayer, not to fault-finding. Let us be clear: there are things that are plainly evil or wicked and to which it would be folly to turn a blind eye. For instance, a woman should not tie herself to an alcoholic and say she did not want to be a fault-finder.

What I'm talking about here is the ability to extend grace. The problem with fault-finding is its consistency, which comes from a position of self-righteousness and setting oneself on a pedestal.

If Adam did not need help, we would not exist. The Bible clearly states that the woman was created not for that international agency job, *chama*, or political appointment, but for the man (1 Corinthians 11:9). Obviously, any human being who needs help is not perfect. I put it to you that the Adam in your life is well aware of his weaknesses. I pray that you do not have a Nabal in your life, but even so, marriage is for keeps and in observing the way Abigail dealt with her husband, even he does not need fault-finding – he needs wisdom. There is a point at which a wife has to step back and allow God to fix what needs to be fixed. Women were created to help their husbands, not to help God.

If you have soberly agreed to be joined to a sensible, God-fearing man, know that any possible fault you can find was paid for at Calvary, and your job is not to point it out, but to be a strengthener – not of the fault, but of the weakness it reveals. To help someone is to give him or her something he or she does not already have, or to point out that which a person has but is not aware he or she possesses.

A critical spirit cost Michal the gift of motherhood. Be very careful, because God takes *very* seriously the way we handle His sons' hearts.

7

May God keep you from a marriage definable only in complex Kiswahili.

Even the happiest marriages face tough challenges. If you are single, know that the prayer of prevention is better than the prayer of cure. This is the time to pray that you are spared from a marriage whose activities are defined by lengthy Kiswahili terms:

> *misukosuko mwaka mzima*
> *songobingo la* report form *za watoto*
> *changamoto za madeni ya Fuliza*
> *kizungumkuti sebuleni*
> *kukuru-kakara za kutumia* tissue
> *segemnege ya* stockings *kichwani*
> *paruwanja la* househelp
> *dugudwa la* pastor
> *zilizala za ma* slaps

If you are married, it is not too late! God is still firmly on His throne. Go boldly before Him and receive mercy and find grace to help you in your time of need (Hebrews 4:16).

God, I am trusting You for:

_____
_____
_____
_____
_____
_____
_____
_____
_____
_____
_____
_____
_____
_____
_____

8

Women are better than men – at being women.

Both secular and evangelical feminists are right; they just never complete this sentence. Women *are* better than men – but only at being women. What a man can do, a woman can do better, but only in regards to womanhood and being a woman. No man can out-woman any woman born of a woman. No matter what a man tries or how he modifies himself, he will never be a woman. It is best for him to remain himself, seeking and walking with Jesus in order for him to be the man God has called him to be.

I feel that I should stress one more time for you, my dear reader, that a woman is only better than a man at being a woman. Many women are richer, more intelligent, wiser, more professionally qualified, more spiritually mature than their husbands. God knows this – He did, after all, create, call and choose them.

Still, in His wisdom, for His Name's sake, and even if because He simply felt like it (He is God! He can do as He pleases; Psalm 135:6!), He decided that in the family structure, the woman will submit to the man. In the church structure, the woman is not to teach, but to remain silent (1 Timothy 2:12). It does not make the man better than she is; it does not make her worse than he is. Many feel that Peter calling us "the weaker vessel" (1 Peter 3:7) is an insult, but think about this example that the late Adrian Rogers gave: silk is weaker than canvas. Which is more costly? Which would people rather own? "Weaker", then, does not necessarily mean "less precious than".

If you doubt my view regarding women as pastors, I challenge you to name five women who were pastors between the time of Jesus' resurrection and the year 1850. Ponder that against 1 Timothy 2 and 2 Timothy 3. Think about 1 Timothy 2:12 and Titus 2:3-5. I'm also happy to hear your interpretation of 1 Timothy 3:2, which tells us that an overseer must be above reproach, the husband of one wife.

Dear woman, accept your femininity. It is beautiful. There is so much we can accomplish as women if we stop peeking over the fence at what men are doing and accomplishing and saying, and focus on being excellent in the role God gave us.

9

Men are better than women - at being men.

The same applies here. No man can out-woman any woman. Why bother if any tries? It is folly that leads to a failure whose revelation is simply a matter of time. It is in our best interest to stick to our lanes.

There are things that men can do better than women, and that is okay.

God decided to create us as women because He saw it fit to do so. There is no need to compete in a playing field in which fair rules disqualify us before the competition starts.

It is best for women to remain themselves, not being clamorous or dramatic or constantly trying to outdo men in the home and elsewhere. We must seek and walk with Jesus in order for us to be the women He has called us to be. Anything else will cause unnecessary misery.

As I prayerfully ponder what it is to be a godly woman, I realize:

_____
_____
_____
_____
_____
_____
_____
_____
_____
_____
_____
_____
_____
_____
_____

10

Invest into eternity.

I once heard a woman say: "The only thing we have on earth that we can take with us to heaven is people."

Isn't it interesting, though, how much weight people put on, how much effort people put towards, things that cannot be carried from time into eternity?

Of what use is your career if your child does not know Jesus?

Of what use is the international agency job if it keeps you away from your husband?

Of what use is the *chama* money if all you do to get it is gossip?

Of what use is your title if your name is not in the Book of Life?

Of what use are your trophies if Jesus is not saying "Well done"?

Of what use is your devotional ministry if your own daily devotions are suffering?

Of what use are the packed pews if the souls that fill them are piled for damnation? God forbid!

Of what use is your giving if you have no love, if it is just for show, or if it is unclean money?

Of what use is a car that cannot drive through heaven's gates?

> *Lay not up for yourselves treasures upon earth, where moth and rust doth corrupt, and where thieves break through and steal: But lay up for yourselves treasures in heaven, where neither moth nor rust doth corrupt, and where thieves do not break through nor steal: For where your treasure is, there will your heart be also.* (Matthew 16:19-21.)

> *Though I speak with the tongues of men and of angels, and have not charity*, I am become as sounding brass, or a tinkling cymbal. And though I have the gift of prophecy, and understand all mysteries, and all knowledge; and though I have all faith, so that I could remove mountains, and have not charity, I am nothing. And though I bestow all my goods to feed the poor, and though I give my body to be burned, and have not charity, it profiteth me nothing.* (1 Corinthians 13:1-3.)

11

God is the only Constant in this ever-changing life.

This quote came from the social media page of a friend I made in 2005 or thereabouts. When I read it, I realized just how much sense it makes. Life is constantly changing. People, careers, seasons, preferences, locations, appearance, trends, cultures rarely remain completely consistent. In all this, however, God remains the same.

Yesterday, today, forever – regardless of what is going on, He can be trusted to be Himself. Isn't that comforting?

I am the LORD, I change not. Jesus Christ the same yesterday, and to day, and for ever. (Malachi 3:6a, Hebrews 13:8.)

God, thank You for:

_____
_____
_____
_____
_____
_____
_____
_____
_____
_____
_____
_____
_____
_____
_____

12

Nobody – not even angels – will do on your behalf what God has commanded you to do.

There are things no angel will do for you, because in commanding you to do them, God has enabled you to do them.

God gives us commands throughout scripture; many of them repeated. *Be strong and of a good courage. Trust in the Lord with all your heart. Get wisdom, and get understanding. Arise. Shake yourself from the dust. Go into all the world, and make disciples. Submit yourselves to God. Resist the devil. Be strong in the LORD and in the power of His might.*

It has wisely – and perhaps also widely – been said that God's commandments are His enablements. As He says it, His power is sent forth for its accomplishment. He is with us and He empowers us by His grace to do what He has told us to do. "Rise up and walk!" is both a command and an enablement. "Fear not!" is both a command and an enablement. "Trust Me!" is both a command and an enablement. There is nothing God commands us to do that He will leave us on our own to struggle with in our own strength. He is right there with us, and while that does not mean there will be no challenges, He will continue to be with us, strengthen us, win for us, win in us, as we walk with and trust in and yield to Him.

Many times, women wallow in misery because they are waiting for God to do certain things for them when He has already given them the power to do it themselves.

It is possible, and within your reach, and your responsibility, while still focusing on God, to participate in and fulfill what He has called and empowered you to do. The power and grace are of Him, and all the glory is to Him. But we must obey.

Many, like the man by the pool of Bethesda in John 5, are being carried by that which should be carrying them (see 13).

Angels will not preach the gospel and make disciples. YOU must.

Angels will not resist the devil on your behalf. YOU must.

Angels will not shake you from the dust — YOU must.

13

Do not allow that which you should carry to carry you.

Jesus gave a threefold command to the man by the pool of Bethesda, in John 5:
Arise.
Take up your mat.
Walk.

Today's woman might apply it thus:

Arise – Get up from that complacent position. Ditch mediocrity and run to Jesus. You are not here to do pedicures and gossip endlessly. There is a call on your life, and it is primarily to love God with all your heart, soul and mind (and your neighbor as yourself); secondarily to love, respect, and serve your husband, and finally to raise the children with whose stewardship you have been entrusted, in order that they may glorify God. Regardless of your marital status, that initial primary call is a must; and if you have children, you will be accountable for who raises them.

Pick up your mat – Feelings, emotions, and influences should not control you. Do not sit there remembering the toothpick that your house help stole from you on that day when it rained heavily in 1972. Stop reflecting on the many ways in which your husband offended and embarrassed you when he forgot to put down the toilet seat at 3:15:07pm on your birthday in 1923. If, like the man by the pool, you realize that you have been sitting in a self-piteous mire of any flavor, waiting for a man to guide you to your healing, I say to you today, enough is enough. Renew your mind. Be transformed. A godly woman is forward-looking and forward-moving. No [woman], setting her hand to the plow, and looking back, is fit for the kingdom of God (Luke 9:62). Unforgiveness definitely should not hold you back, because God does not forgive those who do not forgive (Matthew 6:14-15).

Temperance (self-control) is a component of the fruit of the Spirit. To avoid going back to complacency, mortify the works of the flesh – ruthlessly (Romans 8:13). Your job should not "carry" your life, swaying everything and causing you to force even your prayer life and your family to revolve around it. You dare not let PMS "carry" your moods from one end of a pendulum to another. And is it a pregnancy that carries a woman or a woman that carries a pregnancy? So does it make sense to ask for fried water and the smell of soapy tangerines just because you are pregnant?

Forgive that girl who did not share her *Bournvita* with you when you were in high school. Forgive the coworker who lied. Forgive the ex who mistreated you – or treated you so well and then abruptly left. Forgive anyone against whom you have any hard feelings.

As a final example, no woman should be found lying on the mat of *self* – selfishness, self-esteem, self-confidence, self-help (there is no such thing), self-aggrandizement. Let women be self-aware and have self-control. No woman is self-made. And no matter what – and I know you know what I mean when I say that, because women go through a lot! - no woman should feel self-pity. Arise! Pick up that mat! And…

Walk! – in the light (1 John 1:7). While you have the light (John 12:35). In the Spirit (Galatians 5:16). Circumspectly (Ephesians 5:15). With the wise (Proverbs 13:20).

Drop, with immediate effect, any bad habit, feeling or worldly possession that you have allowed to carry you. Don't you dare attempt to "drop" your husband or children with the excuse that they are holding you back. Any "back" that a godly husband holds you is "back" where you are supposed to be. If you think your husband is cold, remember hell is hot. Choose one temperature. And should there be any burdens that are distracting you from your calling, I remind you of the admonition in Hebrews 12:1:

Lay aside every weight, and the sin which doth so easily beset…and… run with patience the race.

God, please help me to:

_____
_____
_____
_____
_____
_____
_____
_____
_____
_____
_____
_____
_____
_____
_____
_____

14

<u>Someone</u> will raise your children.

Children cannot raise themselves; they *must* be raised. It is up to you as a mother to decide whether you, your TV, the internet, teachers, house helps, the neighbors' children, the streets, strangers, Sabbath School, Sunday School, Vacation Bible Study, or Word of Life camps will raise yours.

Of this one thing be sure, regardless of your choice: you *will* be accountable before God for your role in their lives during their formative years. Decide early what your priorities will be between your job and your children; your new boyfriend and your children; the club and your children; people's opinions and your children; your Ph.D. and your children; your hair and your children; your friends and your children; *Top 40 Under 40* and your children. Should anything happen to your children because you entrusted them to strangers so that you could chase a career, please know that you will be accountable.

In a world that looks down on Biblical motherhood, it can be difficult to make and stick to the choice to do what you can, by God's grace, to raise your children right. Know that God, who gives grace, is by your side, and report to Him daily for strength to be who He has called you to be. Remember that you will give an account before Him.

Lo, children are an heritage of the LORD, and the fruit of the womb is His reward (Psalm 127:3).

15

A one-second "No" or "Go" from the Holy Spirit can keep a woman from a lifetime of pain.

God made life simple*, and loves to speak to us. He is concerned about our walk and our choices. He will not hesitate or refuse to guide or instruct us if we genuinely go to Him, ready to obey what He says.

Two examples demonstrate the importance of seeking God before making a decision. The first is Joshua, when approached by the Gibeonites, as seen in Joshua chapter 9. Because Joshua did not pray before making a decision, he was tricked into making a covenant that he would not destroy a nation God had instructed should be destroyed.

The second is David, before each battle. "Shall I go up?" He asked the Lord, each time. The instructions were not identical. But he obeyed each time, and that was the secret to his victory.

Is there a project you would like to start? A man who has proposed? An item you are considering buying?

Pause and listen. Ask God what to do. Obey Him, for not only does He know the future; He also forever has your best interests at heart.

*"Simple" is not necessarily synonymous with "easy".

16

The virtuous woman will do her husband good and not evil all the days of her life.

That is what Proverbs 31 tells us. This means she will do him good and not evil before she meets or knows him, when he offends her, if his life is marred by scandal, if she discovers a terrible secret about him, if he is spiritually less mature, and regardless of his pocket. Because it speaks of her life and not his, it also means that she will not malign or disgrace his name even if she is widowed.

You see, from this, how important it is for women to carry themselves appropriately, discreetly and prudently before marriage, and to pray fervently before agreeing to be united to a man for life. It is difficult enough for human beings to do good, just once, even to good people. Imagine how difficult it is for a woman to do good, all the days of her life, to a man who does not love her as commanded in scripture; to a Nabal, a crude and mean man whose name itself means "fool" (1 Samuel 25:3); or to an unbeliever with whom the yoke is unequal and thus very uncomfortable, at the very least, and painfully damaging to the neck, at worst.

17

God – not my education, not my family, not my research, not science, not a god, not the government, not the universe, not books – *will show me the path of life.*

In His Presence – not in a bar, or in my self-esteem, or in Kamau's arms, or in Ikechukwu's car, or in my job, or in my marriage, or in my child, or in singleness, or in cake, or in sex, or in human rights, or in America – i*s fullness of joy.*

At His right hand – only! not at the club, not at the crack of dawn, not at a graduation ceremony, not at a distant time yet to come, not at a church, not at a bank, not at a wedding ceremony, not at standard conditions of temperature and pressure – *are pleasures for evermore* (Psalm 16:11).

Heavenly Father, please forgive me for seeking solace, advice, joy and pleasure in:

_____
_____
_____
_____
_____
_____
_____
_____
_____
_____
_____
_____
_____
_____
_____

18

God is the God of our narrow escapes.

God, who delivers us from the snare of the fowler (Psalm 91:3), is the God who rescues us when we are in danger. No narrow escape is a coincidence. There are dangers from which God has rescued us that we do not even know about. No evil you have escaped has been escaped without His rescue. It is wise to be conscious of this, for it will foster gratitude.

He has given his angels charge over thee, to keep thee in all thy ways (Psalm 91:11).

God, thank you for rescuing me from:

_____
_____
_____
_____
_____
_____
_____
_____
_____
_____
_____
_____
_____
_____
_____
_____

19

Forgive freely, considering the state in which you'd find yourself if Jesus were to withhold His forgiveness from you.

In Genesis 1, we are told that human beings were created in the image of God. That means that there are certain things, such as injustice, that human beings can sense immediately, Christian or not.

I was in a restaurant with a lady and her one-and-a-half-year-old son (let's call him Liam), who was fast asleep in her arms. A plate of fries had been ordered for him, but he woke up just as we were about to leave. We asked the waitress to pack his food. She nodded and left, and Liam tasted about two fries, only for her to return and whisk his plate away.

The look on his face was one of utter disbelief and anger. Immediately, his mother and I burst out laughing. But the look held for a few seconds. His shocked scowl seemed to be saying, "Did that just happen? How dare she!"

It was a brief moment before he burst into tears, which stopped as soon as the waitress returned his fries neatly wrapped in foil.

Liam, even at his age, felt that something had happened that was not right. As adults, we understand this as well, perhaps even better. That same feeling - "Did that just happen? How dare s/he!" – is not uncommon when an injustice of any sort occurs.

The child forgot about it within minutes (no wonder Jesus says in Matthew 18:3 that we should become like little children!), and will probably laugh along with whoever tells him the story, if it is told to him when he is older, but many times, as people grow older, their record-keeping skills grow stronger. The flesh resists laying offenses aside, as one person said. It cries out for vengeance, be it for a stolen pencil or a broken marriage.

There are two challenges to this tendency, however. Firstly, we must forgive. It is a command. God says clearly that forgiveness will be held from us if we withhold it from others (Matthew 6:15).

Secondly, we cannot forgive unless we accept Jesus and surrender to Him, kill the flesh and choose His way. Forgiveness, then, is not about willpower or experience. It is purely by God's grace. It is a godly attribute.

We have all sinned, and any sin we commit deserves from God more punishment than we could possibly personally mete to those who offend us. When Jesus died for us, the wrath - that severe wrath for even our tiniest sins, but also for our most grievous - was poured out on Him in full. If Jesus could take our sin upon Himself, and if God could forgive us, how dare we hold anyone's sin against them? As difficult as it may be, we must forgive.

Not forgiving also has a final problem: it could be blasphemous. We do not know whether those who sinned against us have gone before God, like the tax collector in the temple in Luke 18:13, pounded their chests in sorrow, and said, "God, be merciful to me, a sinner." We do not know if they have sought forgiveness from God.

If God has forgiven a person, but we choose not to, we are saying, in essence, that our unforgiveness trumps and is more superior to God's forgiveness. That is a blasphemous risk no human being should dare to take.

Jesus made it clear in teaching us to pray that as we beg Him to forgive us our ten thousand talents owed, we had better be sure we have forgiven our fellow servants their hundred pence debt to us (Matthew 18:21-35).

What is owed to you? Of how much more importance is it than the debt Jesus paid for you? If your husband is cold, hell is hot!

It is difficult, but forgive. And in so doing, remember one person you must also forgive, if sins have been confessed and forsaken: **YOURSELF**.

And forgive us our debts, as we forgive our debtors (Matthew 6:12).

I forgive:

_____
_____
_____
_____
_____
_____
_____
_____
_____
_____
_____
_____
_____
_____
_____
_____

20

Every single sin can be traced to one of two things: fear or pride.

Think about it.

Abortion is a result of perhaps the worst form of pride any human being can have. Unfortunately, the reason behind the pregnancy or the way in which it happened does not give any woman the right to terminate it. Stop, drop and roll, and you will realize that no matter what anybody says, the reasons for abortion, syrupy sweet though they may be phrased, are simply:

- I don't want to have to deal with the father of this baby
- I don't want to have to share my money
- I don't want to have to share my time or give up my comforts
- I'm concerned about what people will think of me
- I was taken advantage of, and need control
- I deserve to enjoy my life without any consequences
- I refuse to bear the child of a rapist

Abuse is pride – it is a person communicating that they have more value than those they abuse.

Adultery is pride – it is similar to abuse. It also comes from a sense that nobody can see what is done and therefore nothing will happen, which flouts Psalm 139. Adultery can sometimes also become blatant, as a man or woman says to his or her spouse, "So what? Do what you will – I don't care that you know."

Alcoholism is the fear of facing and/or living in reality and/or dealing with issues. It can also be classified among things that make up "the pride of life" (1 John 2:16).

Anxiety is fear – it is even a synonym for it. Simply put, it is a concern and even sometimes a belief that God will not come through, which is a lie.

Atheism is *extreme* pride. The issue with atheism, God once revealed to me, is not facing the reality that God is, but having to let go of sin. This type of pride is foolish (Proverbs 14:1 and 53:1). Note that the fool says in his *heart* that there is no God. It is important to realize, especially in these last days, that his *mouth* may shout it in pulpits, his songs may sing that there is a God, but his fruit demonstrates where his *heart* truly is.

Divorce is often pride. It is simply the refusal of one or both parties to forgive.

Fornication is pride – refusing to wait for the appointed time for sex to happen, or deciding that one's own shallow, superficial, myopic, humanistic, and easily destructible "commitment" holds more weight than God's wisdom and command to marry.

Gluttony is probably both pride and fear. Pride, in that there is plenty and moderation is thrown out of the window; fear because one wants to taste everything or feels food might run out.

Guilt is fear – it is a person saying, "I have done injustice, and it must be avenged."

Homosexuality is pride. God made human beings a certain way. To refuse to be that way, regardless of inclinations, is sin. To say "I can't help it" is no different from a thief saying "I have to steal".

Lying is fear that if one tells the truth, something bad will happen. It can also be a pride that assumes the person or people being lied to is/are less intelligent than the liar.

Self-pity and anything that glorifies the self is pride.

Serving false gods is pride – where a human being shakes his or her fist at God because of impatience or a state of life with which one is angry.

Strife is a result of pride – *only by pride cometh contention* (Proverbs 13:10).

Theft is both fear and pride – fear that if something is not acquired, there will be lack; pride, because the thief feels he deserves what is stolen more than the owner does.

Witchcraft is pride – it is a manifested desire for control, a refusal to yield to God's timing, and a result of envy, jealousy, and rage.

God, deliver me from:

_____
_____
_____
_____
_____
_____
_____
_____
_____
_____
_____
_____
_____
_____
_____
_____

21

The wise woman understands that not all situations are worthy of her commentary, and not all commentary is worthy of her response.

It may very well be worthy of a response - just not hers. (Proverbs 4:7, 31:26).

I need to remain silent when:

_____
_____
_____
_____
_____
_____
_____
_____
_____
_____
_____
_____
_____
_____
_____
_____

22

May the All-Knowing God never say to us, "I never knew you."

Matthew 7:23 is perhaps one of the scariest verses in the Bible, firstly because God is All-Knowing, and so it is possibly the toughest judgment for Him to say He never knew a person, whether literally or metaphorically.

Secondly, this statement will be made one day to those who have been acclaimed by the world as pastors, prophets, philanthropists, people who do "many wonderful works" – to so-called Christians, who have deceived the world but through whom Jesus sees, because not even the thickest darkness can hide our deepest selves from God (Psalm 139:11-12).

Thirdly, Jesus says these people are **many**.

Please know this: God can neither be deceived (Acts 5:1-11) nor mocked (Galatians 6:7). May we never be found among those to whom these terrifying words are said, in Jesus' Name. Amen.

It is a fearful thing to fall into the hands of the living God (Hebrews 10:31).

Knowing God and being known by Him means:

_____
_____
_____
_____
_____
_____
_____
_____
_____
_____
_____
_____
_____
_____

23

The fattest bank account cannot buy you eternal life and the flashiest car cannot drive you into heaven.

Someone dear to me once asked me:

"Even if a person has ten cars, how many can he or she drive at a time? Even if a house has 25 bedrooms, in how many can one sleep at a time?"

Her intent was to highlight the folly of placing too much weight on earthly possessions. Jesus said in Luke 12:15, *Take heed, and beware of covetousness: for a man's life consisteth not in the abundance of the things which he possesseth.*

Never agree to tie your sense of worth to ephemeral things.

I should put my trust in God, and not in:

_____
_____
_____
_____
_____
_____
_____
_____
_____
_____
_____
_____
_____
_____
_____

24

God will not change His word or His character just because you are
in love,
in debt,
in pain, or
in America.

God has made it clear in Malachi 3:6 and in Hebrews 13:8 that He does not change; He is the same yesterday, today and forever.

It does not matter whether you are in a culture where people respect parents or one where they would rather not deal with them. It does not matter how funny the joke is or how angering the insult is.

It does not matter whether your pastor says that times have changed and this is a new dispensation, an unprecedented manifestation, a fresh wine, a revival breaking out, a double portion, a jubilee year, or any other thing. It doesn't matter how sweet the words, how fresh the suit, how acrylic the nails, how high the heels of the person saying or doing things. It does not matter if it rains, shines, snows, thunders:

If what is happening or being said or done is not consistent with scripture, it is not of God, and you must flee from it, discard it, and reject it. Who are you here to please? Man or God? (Galatians 1:10.) Decide now.

25

Pray for your children, even if you are yet to meet them.

In Jeremiah 1:5, God says to Jeremiah that He knew him before He formed him in the womb. In the same way, he knew you and me, and should it be His will for you to have children, He knows them.

Prayerfully seek Him about this, and should he show you that you will be a mother one day, begin to pray for your children. If you are pregnant, prophesy over your children. Speak to them even while they are in the womb. Pray for them. Worship with them. Even babies in the womb recognize the presence of God – the leap or kick will show you that indeed you are praying for a living person.

Research has proven that children pick up on their mothers' dispositions even while they are in the womb. If the mother is stressed, it can stress the baby. If the mother contemplates abortion and then changes her mind, the baby could end up feeling rejected, unless the issue is taken to God in prayer. Joy is, therefore, an advantageous disposition for a pregnant woman, and the best way to ensure it is to be walking with God all the time.

I always say this to women, at the risk of sounding superstitious: our battle is spiritual, but the vessels are human. Pray for your baby every morning and ask God to protect him or her from malice and to protect you both from complications. You may not be able to avoid letting all and sundry touch your womb (although a harsh look and a *Do Not Touch the Bump* t-shirt can go a long way), so be sure to pray. Anybody touching a pregnant belly could be laying hands on the baby. Do not be ignorant of the enemy's devices.

Pray for each child's entire life, continually. Pray for protection against all the vices going on today. Pray for spiritual victory and lives that glorify God.

If you are waiting to meet and hold your baby before you start praying, you will be too late.

Sorry, what? You need to go and do your nails first? May that nail salon close, hike its prices beyond what you can afford or move to another town that your child might be saved, in Jesus' Name.

26

May the Lord keep you from, and keep from you, anything or anyone you cannot let go of for His sake.

Or, in other words, may you so love the Lord that you will not hesitate to let anyone or anything go if He requires that you do so, in Jesus' Name, Amen.

This command found in Mark 12:30 is found in several other chapters in both the Old and New Testaments:

And thou shalt love the Lord thy God with all thy heart, and with all thy soul, and with all thy mind, and with all thy strength: this is the first commandment.

God, today, for Your sake, I ask for Your help as I get rid of:

_____
_____
_____
_____
_____
_____
_____
_____
_____
_____
_____
_____
_____
_____
_____

27

What exactly does your cleavage on the internet have to do with "God is good"?

Does it make any sense to post indecent pictures and "humble brags" on social media or on your phone, for all and sundry to see, and then caption them with scriptures?

While dressing does not guarantee our salvation in any way, it identifies us, and it can encourage our fellow women to either be modest or immodest. Dressing can also cause our brothers to stumble.

Almost 10 years ago when I first wrote a book, I mentioned how a few years prior, I was surprised when the first few search results of a Google search for "decent dressing" were people questioning whether women were totally blameless when it came to the high rape statistics in certain countries. The same search produced different results then and still does today, but I found that initial result disturbing. Why would a search for decent dressing bring up rape statistics? And why did that search result change around the time women began to say that dressing does not in any way impact the rampant rape statistics we see today?

Don't get me wrong, I am not condoning rape under any circumstances. To rape a woman is to violate her in perhaps the worst possible way. No woman deserves to be raped, no matter how she dresses. I had to ask myself, however: *Does this not say something about the stumbling blocks women have been to their brothers?* Paul said in Romans 14:21, *It is good neither to eat flesh, nor to drink wine, nor anything whereby thy brother stumbleth, or is offended, or is made weak.*

Will that Christian brother who follows your social media page be thinking about God's goodness when he sees an indecent picture, regardless of the caption?

Still wondering what I'm talking about? Let us drive this point home:

If you walk into a Kenyan hospital and want to identify the doctor, you look for the man in a white coat with stethoscope around his neck.

If you are lost in Nairobi's Central Business District and need directions, the safest person to ask is a guard, a county council official, or a policeman – and how are they identified? By their uniforms. Even if covered by a trench coat, we can tell from the hat and the baton, or from the neon yellow, who is who.

While waiting for your flight at an airport, or for a guest arriving from a different country, you may see a few men and ladies in polished uniforms walk swiftly past you, calm expressions on their faces, the men's shoes glistening as though deep-fried in coconut oil and the ladies lips painted crimson red. They will all be dragging little suitcases behind them and everyone will be in step in what might appear to be a choreographed march. Who are those? You guessed it - the pilots and flight attendants.

If you visit some Kenyan homes, you will identify the house help by a checked dress – sometimes a white apron as well. While I do not personally agree with this distinction except where a house help has flouted repeated instructions against immodesty, I feel I should share it to stress my point.

If you are watching soccer, you can tell which team is which by the colors they wear. You might not know the names of the teams, but you will know which players belong to the same team.

The referee is the guy in the black and white stripes, blowing a whistle and pulling out red or yellow cards.

The *matatu* conductor is the guy in the maroon trousers.

As soon as a stranger's dressing was described to King Ahaziah, he recognized who it was. "It is Elijah the Tishbite!" he exclaimed.

And [Ahaziah] said unto them, What manner of man was he which came up to meet you, and told you these words?

And they answered him, He was an hairy man, and girt with a girdle of leather about his loins. And he said, It is Elijah the Tishbite (2 Kings 1:7-8).

Dressing was one way in which people recognized John the Baptist not only as a person, but also as the Elijah prophesied by Malachi:

Behold, I will send you Elijah the prophet before the coming of the great and dreadful day of the Lord (Malachi 4:5).

And the same John had his raiment of camel's hair, and a leathern girdle about his loins; and his meat was locusts and wild honey (Matthew 3:4).

And if ye will receive it, this is Elias, which was for to come (Matthew 11:14).

In 2010, I wrote,

> *The fashion industry has been manipulated to promote prostitution. Things are becoming shorter and tighter. There is a type of dressing that is reserved for harlots as we see in Proverbs 7:10, and the enemy is trying to blur the lines between decency and irreverence. Because of human beings' love for the expensive, all one has to do to promote evil is hike up its price.*

It's much worse now. And thus the expensive bikini is splashed online with a supposedly spiritual quote that would not convince even the most gullible.

We know that God is good. Say it again with some clothes on, and maybe we will take you seriously.

God sees my innermost motives. I need to keep that in mind when:

28

Marriage is not a piece of paper.

The marriage <u>certificate</u> is a piece of paper. Fragile though it be, that paper can represent solidity. Light though it be, it carries immense weight. Insignificant though it appear, it announces a covenant that can have eternal impact. It is a written symbol of a union created with the first human beings, sealed by God, and backed by heaven.

Wherefore they are no more twain, but one flesh. What therefore God hath joined together, let not man put asunder (Matthew 19:6).

Marriage is honourable in all, and the bed undefiled: but whoremongers and adulterers God will judge (Hebrews 13:4).

Marriage is:

_____
_____
_____
_____
_____
_____
_____
_____
_____
_____
_____
_____
_____
_____
_____

29

Our identity <u>determines</u> our character. Our character <u>reveals</u> our identity.

Our identity, according to Webster's Dictionary, is the *sense of self, providing sameness and continuity in personality over time*.

From this we see that identity is different from personality. It determines our personality or character. It is that picture or concept we have of ourselves that dictates what we do on a regular basis.

In other words, what we do and how we behave (personality and character) emanate from who we are (identity) and not the other way around. That is why Jesus said, "By their fruits, you shall know them" (Matthew 7:16, Luke 6:44-45).

By observing what people do, you will know who they are because they cannot act contrary to their identity.

I once watched a Nigerian movie about a princess who was kidnapped by the palace maid. She grew up in the maid's home as the maid's daughter. She lived like a maid and behaved like a maid: subservient, humble, speaking only when spoken to.

One day, the maid called the princess to her side and told her the truth about her heritage. "Go to the palace and tell the king that you are the lost princess," she instructed.

The princess went to the palace and found out that indeed she was the missing daughter of the king. She found out she had a younger sister who now had to train her in the ways of the palace so that she could become fit to be a queen. One day, the

Lost Princess was talking to somebody in the palace when her sister rebuked her harshly. "Why are you bowing your head like a maid?" her sister asked. "Don't you know you are royalty?"

That scene gave me a better understanding of the concept of identity. The princess had no idea that she was royalty, so she acted like she wasn't. When she found out who she was, she was able to lift up her head and walk tall. Don't get me wrong — maids are no less human than princesses. This lady's state would have been just as tragic if she had been a maid who thought she was the queen.

Do you know who you are? Does your character match your true identity?

30

Do not be deceived. There is "My" truth, "Your" truth, and *The* Truth.

And ye shall know the truth, and the truth shall make you free (John 8:32). **Purpose to know the truth.**

Jesus saith unto him, I am the Way, the Truth, and the Life: no man cometh unto the Father, but by Me (John 14:6). **Nobody can come to the Father without the Truth.**

Sanctify them through Thy truth: Thy word is truth (John 17:17). **May you be sanctified by God's truth.**

Which truth are you speaking, believing or living? Choose wisely.

Jesus, I need Your help with:

_____
_____
_____
_____
_____
_____
_____
_____
_____
_____
_____
_____
_____
_____
_____

31

God is the God even of the desperate.

Do not let anyone shame you for being single, for wanting to be married, or for asking them to join you in praying for a spouse or a child or a job or finances or a miracle of any sort. The dictionary defines this kind of desperation as *having a great need or desire for something*.

God is YOUR GOD. His ears are open to your cry. If they call you "desperate," know you are in good company, as we will see from the examples below.

The Bible is full of desperate people. Here are just a few. It is important for women to be scripture-literate. Take this list as a challenge to get to know about the situations each of these people faced by seeking them out in your Bible:

- Abraham with no seed.
- Lot in Sodom.
- Joseph in prison.
- The Israelites as slaves in Egypt.
- The Israelites at the Red sea.
- Rahab, making a deal for her family.
- Gideon, on being called.
- Samson, on his last day.

- Naomi, widowed and childless in Moab.
- Hannah in the temple.
- The Israelites before Goliath.
- David before Saul, asking Jonathan for confirmation.
- Hezekiah facing the wall.
- The king, up all night, after Daniel was thrown into the lions' den.
- Esther, calling a fast.
- Habakkuk, crying, "How long, Lord??"
- Jonah, in the belly of the whale.
- The woman with the issue of blood.
- Jairus, pleading for his daughter.
- Zacchaeus, scuttling up the sycamore tree.

- JESUS, IN THE GARDEN OF GETHSEMANE, ASKING GOD TO TAKE AWAY THE CUP, BUT YIELDING TO HIS WILL ALL THE SAME.

- The disciples, praying for Peter's release.
- The people in the shipwreck about which Paul had been told.

Do not take the word "desperate" as an insult. Whatever your need may be, cry out to God, lady! If you are wrong in desiring what you desire, He will show you that you are, and He will give you peace.

Trust in Him at all times, you people. Pour out your heart before Him, for God is a Refuge for us (**Psalm 62:8**).

32

May you not use your own mouth or your own internet to destroy your own future.

Be careful, little mouth, what you say.
Be careful, little fingers, what you type.

You are always being watched. God is your Only Relevant Audience and the One to whom you will answer, and nothing can be hidden from Him (Hebrews 4:13).

For by thy words thou shalt be justified, and by thy words thou shalt be condemned (Matthew 12:37).

As I reflect on this, I feel led to:

_____
_____
_____
_____
_____
_____
_____
_____
_____
_____
_____
_____
_____
_____
_____

33

Are you a woman?

I think scripture backs me up when I say that the life of anyone who encounters you should improve simply because they encountered a woman. Countless times since the beginning of this world, God has used women to help men not only survive or improve, but also escape danger and flourish.

The Bible is awash with examples, from Eve to Sarah to Jochebed to Zipporah to Rahab to Deborah to Ruth to Mary to Lydia to Priscilla and many more – of women who rose up for, stepped in to assist, walked with, spoke to, and did so much for men, not in and of themselves, but by God's grace and by His will that they be true helpers. Thank God that the Bible does not hide weaknesses. This shows us that we, too, can each make a positive difference.

And what an honor and a strong message to us that God used a woman to come to earth, and that the resurrected Jesus appeared first to women! This is not a call to evangelical feminism. I am simply imploring you to understand your value, take up your position, and glorify God.

If your husband is at the same job, making the same salary, operating with the same mindset, fighting the same battles, compassing the same mountain – hour after hour, day after day, week after week, month after month, year after year, decade after decade! - did he marry a woman and a help meet?

34

A woman who does not know who she is will act like who she is not.

Every decision we make is a result of the way we see ourselves (and a symptom of our *true* perspective of God). Our identity, or our understanding of it, determines our actions. If you think you're stuck in a rut, or are feeling depressed, covetous, lonely, fearful, regretful, etc., sit down for a moment and ask yourself, "What lie have I believed about myself to bring me to this point?" Talk to Jesus. Understanding how He sees you, and understanding that that's the only truth about yourself, will help you heal.

Cast all your care upon Him, for He cares for you
(1 Peter 5:7).

Fifteen things God says about me in the Bible are:

_____
_____
_____
_____
_____
_____
_____
_____
_____
_____
_____
_____
_____
_____
_____

35

Every man is a leader.

Dear single ladies, that man will lead you somewhere. You need to figure out where he's leading you and jump ship if need be. Pay attention to the Holy Spirit, and listen for that "No" or "Go".

Is he leading you into a closer walk with God?
Is he leading you into marriage?
Is he leading you to his bedroom - or yours?
Is he leading you off a cliff or into a ditch (Luke 6:39)?
Is he leading you nowhere?

Dear married ladies, you are at the point of no return. Your husband, regardless of the type of leader he is, is the head of your home, a position to which he has been appointed by God. Only in **very** few circumstances can you jump ship without risking your eternal destiny (Luke 16:18, Hebrews 13:4b). God is your strength. In His hand is the heart of the king (Proverbs 21:1); how much more your husband's? Call on Him for rescue, if need be. Thank Him for the blessing and grace of being a wife at all times.

As a single woman, I should:

_____
_____
_____
_____
_____
_____
_____
_____
_____
_____
_____
_____
_____
_____
_____

36

Until we solve the quandary of fornication, we will not resolve the quagmire of abortion.

We are living in the last days, and so there are things that will not have global solutions or resolutions. It is going to get a lot worse.

However, that the days are evil and we are living in perilous times does not mean we should hang our boots and silently let evil prevail. Until Jesus returns, there is no deadline for making disciples. It must continue with fervor – and much more fervor than has ever existed in the past. The truth must still be said. It might not be received, but that it was not heard should never be an excuse for those around us.

As you interact with and mentor the younger generation, please ponder the connection between fornication and abortion, and try to advise the youth to avoid the former in order not to have to find themselves contemplating the latter. Set the truth and the reality of their choices before them as happened to the Israelites in Deuteronomy 30.

If you are a young woman living in fornication, please know that the enemy that makes it seem so sweet does not wish you well, and if there were such a thing as perfect hatred, he would hate you with all of it. Flee from the deception that that pleasure is beneficial. It is a dangerous, ephemeral pleasure.

If you have become pregnant outside wedlock, then I would like to beseech you to do three things, immediately, regardless of the circumstances in which you became pregnant:

Firstly, repent, if you fornicated (fornication is simply having sex outside marriage) or committed adultery (which means having sex with a person's spouse or with a man other than your husband) and ask God to forgive you. If you were raped – and I know it may seem easy to type – I beg of you: ask God for the grace to forgive the man or men who violated you and to remove vengeance from your mind. Whatever the situation, ask God to guide you, be with you and keep far from you any person, any doctor, any nurse, any influence that could cause you to consider killing the child He has placed in your womb. Ask Him for help. He will come through for you. Psalm 145:18 says that the Lord is near to those who call upon Him in truth. If God is near you, you will be fine.

Secondly, ask God to lead you to a minimum of three believers you can share your situation with, and ask them not to let you isolate yourself.

Third, do not isolate yourself. If you live alone, please consider either hosting someone close or moving in with someone temporarily. Keep your time occupied. Study scripture and spend time in fellowship.

You have been entrusted with a life, and not only is this a responsibility; it is also an honor and a privilege. Your womb has been entrusted with a baby, even when women all over the world, old and young, are praying for the same, some having prayed for decades. Why you? Should you proceed to murder this baby, you will immediately realize that it is not worth it. I beg of you, do not abort your child. Fornication and abortion are not worth it.

Thou shalt not kill (Exodus 20:13).

Know ye not that the unrighteous shall not inherit the kingdom of God? Be not deceived: neither fornicators... nor adulterers... shall inherit the kingdom of God (1 Corinthians 6:9-10).

If you have already committed these sins, then it is not too late to turn to Jesus and begin to walk with Him. If you haven't repented yet, please go before God immediately and confess your sin to Him, ask for His forgiveness and make the choice to sin no more. Ask Him to guide you through your grief and to comfort you; His Word says in 2 Corinthians 1:3-5 that He is the God of all comfort. Ask Him to keep you from fornication and adultery. He loves you still, and will receive and redeem you.

All that the Father giveth Me shall come to Me; and him that cometh to Me I will in no wise cast out (John 6:37).

God, I am crying out to You today to:

_____
_____
_____
_____
_____
_____
_____
_____
_____
_____
_____
_____
_____
_____
_____

37

How interesting that people are having sex earlier and earlier, and getting married later and later!

This was brought to my attention while I was listening to a sermon some time ago, where the pastor revealed this information and I looked back and realized that it is a fact. The devil has so deceived this generation that people are pushing marriage further and further ahead and starting to have sex earlier and earlier.

As a woman, you cannot control a man, but you can refuse to partner with him in sin. Remember, she who walks with the wise will be wise, but a companion of fools will be destroyed. Choose your friends wisely. Pray that God keeps you from any fool or any man who would violate you, and remember that some situations do not require faith or fights, they require flight. Flee!

Flee also youthful lusts: but follow righteousness, faith, charity, peace, with them that call on the Lord out of a pure heart. (2 Timothy 2:22).

God, show me:

39

The prayer of prevention is better than the prayer of cure.

It is better, and simpler, and even easier, to pray when times are good that we are protected from the bad, than it is to pray during tough challenges that we are delivered from them. Jesus guaranteed in John 16:33 that there would be tribulation in this world. He encouraged us to be of good cheer, for He has overcome the world.

But there are avoidable tribulations. Praying in the morning can prevent a flat tire, or give peace if it happens. Praying before a meeting can invite God into it, circumventing chaos and strife. Prayer before marriage can prevent divorce as God reveals a person's true character and a wedding is cancelled. Prayer before a purchase can keep a person from buying a rotten mango. Prayer before a battle will ensure a valid strategy, leading to victory.

Prayer, glory to God, is that stitch in time that goes down through generations and saves nine.

God, today I seek Your protection from:

_____
_____
_____
_____
_____
_____
_____
_____
_____
_____
_____
_____
_____
_____
_____
_____

40

The prayer of cure is better than no prayer at all.

That a problem has occurred does not mean one should give up or begin to weep as if there is no Balm in Gilead. God is still God, and still firmly on His throne. That means that for a child of God, the worst anything can do is *pretend* it will not be okay.

Even Jonah, in his arguably self-imposed problems in the thick of the seaweed in the belly of the whale, prayed and was succored (Jonah 2).

And we know that all things work together for good to them that love God, to them who are the called according to his purpose (Romans 8:28).

Did you see that? All things. Not some things, many things or most things. For anyone who loves and is called by God, any single thing that can be referred to as a thing must cooperate with every other thing and work for [the] good.

God, please rescue me from:

_____
_____
_____
_____
_____
_____
_____
_____
_____
_____
_____
_____
_____
_____
_____

41

The Proverbs 31 woman did not have a "popping" social life.

Have you ever watched a godly woman above 40 years of age? How many friends does she have? How many events does she attend, if she is not a pastor's wife or in charge of a ministry? What trends does she follow? How often do you even get to see her?

Nowhere in scripture do we see godly women participating in *chamas*, *owambes*, clubbing, hen parties, or anything of the same ridiculously revelrous nature.

Permit me to use broken English in this chapter, because some things require more than grammar.

To the Wander Woman: what is it? Must you have ten friends on each street? Must you be the one people call when they want to know where to have the most fabulous events? Does your kitchen floor have jiggers? Does your couch have lice? God forbid! If not, why can't you stay in one place and serve your husband and spend time with your children? What happened to women simply enjoying their families?

Must you attend every *owambe* for people to understand you are Yoruba? All this your *waka-about*; if elections are happening in Angola, you are an observer. "Yes, the Ambassador's wife is a good friend of mine."

If strangers in a queue crack a joke Amharic, you laugh and respond. "I visited Addis briefly last year, out of curiosity. Beautiful people."

If someone asks about a hashtag, you are the authority. "That not what happened. People are spreading propaganda. It is the woman's fault."

Khoikhoi recipe, *na* you cook *am* pass. "Coincidentally, I lived among the people during my last consultancy. You know, these things we read in textbooks, we need to be very careful how much we imbibe."

Up and down, down and up, from pillar to post to bus stop to airport to balcony to beach to hotel to party. *Abeg*, shift, Wander Woman; can't you see that that your ubiquitous *gele* is blocking traffic? With all this observing and consulting, can you recite Psalm 23 or the Lord's Prayer? Did you preach to any Ambassador or Ethiopian about Jesus?

And you, Madam *Chama* Patron. Must you belong to 25 *chamas* or women's groups? For what? So that you can have money to stick eyelashes on or go to the spa? Even if each *chama* is about investing, how much property must you have for you to feel you have invested enough? Must you have a plot in Isinya, in

Isebania, on Kenyatta Road, in Namanga? Why not invest in eternal things?

What kind of woman is seen every time a town is being opened and another is being closed? Burj Khalifa opening, we see Wander Woman on a celebrity's Instagram profile. Miguna's house vandalized, we see her in the news, standing behind the human rights official. Banana Island party, *na* that her Wander Woman face we go *dey* see for every news outlet. Who is with her children all this time? How are they doing in school? How is their physical, emotional, spiritual health? Does she know whether they are being bullied? Is she sure that she can trust those around them? Does she even *know* her children?

Any woman who is allergic to her home will have a chain-reaction house. A chain reaction house is the type where, should one move a living room cabinet ever so slightly:

"*Shwi-shwi-shwi-shwi*" a gecko will scamper for safety, accidentally alarming a bird;

"*Kwiiii! Dudu! Mwenekudi!*" the bird will disown its nest behind the cabinet, almost entering people's eyes as it flies out of the woodworks, exposing a mouse;

"Squeak! *Kir-krr-krr-krr-krr*", the mouse will hurriedly retreat into its new residence, running over a guest's feet;

"*Uuuuwiii!*" the guest will scream and jump back, waking up a mosquito;

"*Ng'wiiiiiiiiiiii...*" the mosquito will buzz irritably and bite someone.

Women who serve God hardly have time to have hundreds of "friends" or make quarterly pilgrimages to Israel to take selfies at the garden tomb and Capernaum or pose on hotel balconies in Rome and Mombasa. Jesus is risen, in case you did not see the sign or read the verse. He is close to you everywhere you go.

The only woman similar to this in scripture is the woman in Proverbs 7, and it is not a compliment to be compared to her.

She is loud and stubborn; her feet abide not in her house: Now is she without, now in the streets, and lieth in wait at every corner. (Proverbs 7:11-12.)

Let your feet find it comfortable to abide in your house. If there are jiggers, fumigate. Enjoy the company of the man who married you and the children you bore him. Up-and-down is not comely for a woman. Stay home and keep a clean house. I urge you to help bring in an income as well. Do not wear property in the name of Chanel bags or use money that could help your family on a first-class ticket to join nonsense activities. Even if you have a house help, your supervision is needed. A house with many guests or many children can never be completely neat or spick-and-span, but chain reaction houses can cause malaria. Be careful!

42

Marriage is a gift, not an award or reward for "arrival".

Do not feel less loved by God if you are not married (or more loved than Him if you are!). View this as being about Him, and not about you, and it will affect your perspective not only positively, but also immensely. Marriage is a serious battle (see 37 and 38), so it is not a surprise that many women are staying single longer these days.

But, daughter of God, do not let anyone in this world tell you that you are not good enough to be married because you have not done enough to be marryable. Jezebel and Delilah were wives. The former was married until death did them part. That alone debunks any theory that all married women are women of good and "holy" standing.

You are loved by God, and that is that. He hears your cry and your longings. Talk to Him. He will comfort and answer you.

Fifteen things a wife can carry to the marriage potluck are:

_____
_____
_____
_____
_____
_____
_____
_____
_____
_____
_____
_____
_____
_____
_____

43

There is no shame in wanting to be married.

If they call you "desperate", remind both them and yourself that God is the God of even of the desperate.

It is, in these last days, where people are lovers of themselves (1 Timothy 3:2) and have consciences seared with iron (1 Timothy 4:2), a noble and commendable thing to desire to be a wife. Feel no shame.

As I reflect on this, God, You are showing me that:

_____
_____
_____
_____
_____
_____
_____
_____
_____
_____
_____
_____
_____
_____
_____

44

Marriage is a potluck, not a jackpot.

It would do every woman well to remove from her mind that marriage is about taking herself to someone's house to put her feet up and enjoy "enjoyment". Please also discard, with immediate effect, the notion that marriage is a give-and-take or a fifty-fifty deal. It is not. Marriage is a give-and-give. And as has wisely been said, it is 100%-100%. It is two becoming one.

Marriage is work. That is why you look at married, godly men and say you are waiting for a husband like one of them. That shine you see is the favour that God has brought him on finding a wife. It is the work that He has used her to do on this man. If she pulled you aside and told you what he was like when she met him, you would probably run to River Road to look for that guy you gave the wrong number. Remember him? The one who "cannot even" afford a car, mixes up his L's and R's, smells of a *sukumawiki* stall and has a dirty backpack? Yes, him. The guy with the oversized, mismatched, *achwiti* suit and "sharp-shooter" faux-alligator shoes.

Before you hate on your man's inability to do or own or say some things, please pause for a moment and ask yourself what prayers you have said for him. If you are truly a woman of God, certain things in a man's life need to begin to improve instantly just by virtue of your presence.

A godly woman will inspire her man to get his act together (not by badgering or giving instructions!). She will come into marriage armed with strength for the battle, prayers for the dark nights, and comfort for the troubles. If you have been with this man for three years and *nothing* in his life has improved, he is not the problem – you are. Yes! If things – especially spiritually! – are worse because of your presence, that is wickedness. It is coldhearted to demoralize a man and deplete the little he has when all he needs is help.

If a woman is in a relationship right now and her focus is a 15-bridesmaid destination wedding that costs more than her rent for the next year (so that she, with her sh. 28,000 salary, can outdo her friend, the minister's daughter who mints that much in about a day) then this, of course, is her prerogative.

She should not cry when, one month after her wedding, she and her husband are fighting because the sh. 15,000 rent is due, but after collecting all their combined 20-shilling coins and sweeping the entire house to find one 5-shilling coin and one old kernel of roast maize, they can only come up with sh. 7,525.05.

45

Mwanamke anayesinzia
Atashindwa kushikilia;
Na akosaye kupalilia,
Atajifunza kuvumilia.

Men – real men – are an endangered species for which women pray and fast daily. If you are married to one, **shikilia** (hold on to him). If you birth one, **palilia** (nurture him). If not, your life might end up being **kuvumilia** (perseverance or longsuffering, due to the consequences).

May this type of *kuvumilia* never be your portion, in Jesus' Name. Amen.

I need to wake up and start:

_____
_____
_____
_____
_____
_____
_____
_____
_____
_____
_____
_____
_____
_____

46

It takes a woman to prevent a woman.

Just one woman can reduce a man to a piece of bread. Raise each of your sons right and pray for them, because no matter how much school fees you pay, how successful a man becomes, or even how spiritual he grows to be, just one of your fellow women - just one - can reduce him to nothing.

For by means of a whorish woman a man is brought to a piece of bread: and the adulteress will hunt for the precious life. (Proverbs 6:26.)

Mothers can raise good sons by:

_____
_____
_____
_____
_____
_____
_____
_____
_____
_____
_____
_____
_____
_____
_____

Later, your husband might log in to a social media account, share a picture of the meal, and state how pleasantly surprised he is that you cooked for him.

Please do not be discouraged. Try to laugh at yourself a little. They will soon get used to it. It is a wonderful opportunity to discuss what the Bible says about the topic, and can be an amazing witness to your whole family.

However, if you are not yet married, purpose now to submit to your husband, no matter what. Begin to talk to God about it, because submission can be difficult. But with Him, all things are possible. (Matthew 19:26, Mark 10:27.)

As I turn the pages of my Bible, I realize that the true meaning of submission is:

_____
_____
_____
_____
_____
_____
_____
_____
_____
_____
_____
_____
_____
_____
_____
_____

48

Our actions affect more people than just us.

In Joshua 7, we learn about a man named Achan, who fought among the Israelites in the battle of Jericho. God had commanded nobody in Jericho be spared except a harlot known as Rahab, who had hidden Israelite spies and that no spoil be taken from Jericho. God warned in Joshua 16:18-19 that anyone who tried to bring back anything from Jericho would cause trouble in the Israelite camp.

The battle went well and everyone went home, only for the Israelites to be thrashed severely in the next battle. Joshua, the leader, sought God, and it turned out that a man named Achan had taken gold, silver and a robe from Jericho and hidden them in his tent. His actions troubled Israel, as God warned.

The point to note for the purposes of this quote is that when Achan was discovered, not only was he stoned - his entire family was, as well. God is just, and so we know that there must have been a valid reason for this.

Not only did Achan bring trouble upon an entire nation; his actions also gravely affected his wife and children.

It is imperative that we be conscious of the reality that the things we do can affect more than just us.

38

Do not let your fellow woman drive you out of the home God gave you.

If you think your marriage will not be fought, you are in for a surprise and I urge you to wake up, get up and crawl out of that thick fog immediately. Marriage represents the relationship between Christ and His church. It is therefore in the enemy's interest that this institution is as distorted as possible in as many homes as possible for as many generations as possible.

Trials *will* come. But do not ever be so discouraged that you see yourself as a grasshopper in the eyes of any enemy of your home. In Numbers 13:33, the spies said to Moses,

"We saw the giants, the sons of Anak, which come of the giants: and we were in our own sight as grasshoppers, and so we were in their sight."

The word "so" means "also" or "the same", but it can also mean "therefore". In my view, all are plausible meanings in this verse. It is only when you are a grasshopper in your own sight that any adulteress will find the guts to try to squeeze you under her shoes. A woman who thinks she is a grasshopper will act like a grasshopper and will be approached and addressed as is appropriate for a grasshopper. Hear me on this: the battle is spiritual, as Paul tells us in Ephesians 6:12. You must realize who you are as a child of God if you are to prevail in this battle.

For as long as you are married before God, do not let a woman drive you out of your home. Your marriage is a covenant instituted in the beginning, sealed by God, backed by heaven. Pray it through. You *will* prevail. God will give you the wisdom to know when to act as He provides strategies that you implement with success…

Blessed be the Lord my strength which teacheth my hands to war, and my fingers to fight (Psalm 144:1).

…and when to hold your peace as He fights for you, like He did for the Israelites in Exodus 14:14.

49

Suffering is not always humility or nobility.

In fact, sometimes it is a result of the sin of pride, particularly where people enjoy sympathy. I am saddened each time I see a woman putting up with something she does not have to deal with, simply because she is convinced that it means she is being humble.

It's very okay to ask for adjustments where you feel they are needed, or even to request that your needs be met or rights considered. If your chair at work is uncomfortable, say something. If you would like to change your hours slightly in order to spend time with your family, say something. If you are uncomfortable with something your in-laws do, mention it respectfully to your husband. If you feel you have put in enough work at your job to get a raise, mention it.

Something might be able to be done about your situation. Women in the Bible asked. In 2 Kings 4, we are told that a woman went to Elisha one day, saying that her husband had passed on and left her in debt, and her children were on the verge of becoming slaves in order for that debt to be paid. She needed urgent help, and so she went to the man of God. "Your servant feared the Lord," she reminded Elisha.

The prophet asked if she had anything.

She had nothing in her house, she informed him, "save a pot of oil."

"Go, borrow the vessels abroad of thy neighbors, even empty vessels; borrow not a few. And when thou art come in, thou shalt shut the door upon thee and upon thy sons, and shalt pour out into all those vessels, and thou shalt set aside that which is full."

She did as instructed and the one pot filled all the borrowed vessels, until she asked her son for one more and was informed that they were all full. She went to the prophet with that information.

"Go," he told her; "sell the oil, and pay thy debt, and live thou and thy children of the rest."

What if she had been too afraid to ask? The daughters of Zelophehad (Numbers 26) asked, and their land was apportioned to them. Bathsheba asked (1 Kings 1:15-31), and her son got the kingdom. Hannah asked, and she got a son.

Do not be afraid to ask.

Ask the Lord, and prayerfully ask the people He has sent to you.

The worst that can happen is that people will say "No". But at least you will have tried.

50

Do your best not to become so familiar with the blessings for which you prayed, or the God who gave them to you, that you begin to regard both Him and them with contempt.

Has the child you fasted and prayed about become so familiar that you now dare to take out your anger on him or her?

Has the husband you fasted and prayed about become so commonplace that you now dare to call him useless?

Has the job you begged God for now become worthless?

Has your husband been a Bishop so long that you both have the courage to call it *your* church?

Is that money so common now that you have started to trample those to whom you are supposed to share it and look down on those who are in what was your situation just a few years, months, days ago?

Are you now "too saved" to live a holy life?

Are you now so revered by men that you feel no need to seek and thank your God?

Be careful.

47

Let your submission to your husband not come as a surprise.

Well, if you are married and have not been submissive to your husband, then it will be a surprising and new experience for him if you commit to obeying God's command to respect and submit to him. Do not let that make you feel embarrassed. Better late than never.

A lady once shared how she decided one day that going forward, she would treat her husband like the king of his home. As she was setting the table for his lunch, their son passed by and asked if they were expecting visitors. She said she was setting the table for his dad, and he burst out laughing.

If your children are comfortable and expressive around you, they might laugh at you.

"Mom, do we have visitors?" Sarah might whisper, not too different from the example above, as she enters the kitchen, her brother Abraham tiptoeing behind her.

"No, why?" You might ask.

"We just heard you welcoming someone," Abe might say, also trying to whisper. "Have they gone?"

"No, that's your dad," you might reply.

"Hahaaaaaaaa!!!"

If they both burst out laughing and Abe doubles up and rolls on the floor, do not be discouraged. The questions might continue:

"*Kumbe* you know how to cook? You're cooking for Dad?"

"You were asking Dad about his day, like he's a visitor?"

"*Maendeleo!*" Sarah might clap.

"*Maajabu!*" Abe might respond.

"*Miujiza!*" Sarah might try to continue the joke.

"Tom! *Hebu* come and see, *ati* Mom is cooking for Dad!" Abe might say, running off, still laughing.

"Dad! *Ati* Mom is cooking for you today?" Sarah might shout, heading for your living room.

"Hahaaaaa!" A doubting Tom's baritone laugh might reverberate from his room.

51

You are not the only one who can see that you have a good husband. And if you think your husband is cold, know that hell is hot. Pick a temperature.

If in your house there exists a treasure known as **husband,** guard this treasure jealously. Most know its worth, many pray for it, and some think you don't deserve it, yet God gave it to **you**.

How will you handle this treasure?

Today, I will apologize to my husband for:

_____
_____
_____
_____
_____
_____
_____
_____
_____
_____
_____
_____
_____
_____

52

No rings attached means no strings attached.

Until a man commits to marrying you and does so before God and witnesses, he has no right to have any privileges that a husband can access.

No man who has not married you has the right to ask you for sex.

No man who has not married you has any right to your wifely submission. Ephesians 5 commands each wife to submit to her own husband. For as long as he has not married you, for all you know, he could be someone else's future husband.

No man who has not married you or, at the very least, made it clear that this is his goal in the near future, has the right to question your desire to end a relationship with him and begin one with another person.

Any man who wants wifely privileges must face responsibility, honor your God-given dignity, respect your time, and become your husband.

Until then, he has no right to make the same demands as a husband, and it would be foolish to give any such privileges to him.

For this is the will of God, even your sanctification, that you should abstain from fornication... every one of you should know how to possess [her] vessel in sanctification and honor.
(1 Thessalonians 4:3-4.)

53

Sow a wind, reap a whirlwind.

Do not ruin a home unless you are prepared to reap - full measure, pressed down, shaken together, running over, poured into your bosom by your fellow human beings with the same measure you used to pour it out. It is a principle of scripture,

Give, and it shall be given unto you; good measure, pressed down, and shaken together, and running over, shall men give into your bosom. For with the same measure that ye mete withal it shall be measured to you again (Luke 6:38).

When people reject what is good, like Israel is said to have done in Hosea 8, they will plant wind and reap a whirlwind. No matter how many allies evil people acquire to themselves, God will one day soon gather them together for judgment. No woman should do to others that whose whiff alone will cause her to faint (Matthew 7:12, Luke 6:31).

This reminder shows me that:

_____
_____
_____
_____
_____
_____
_____
_____
_____
_____
_____
_____
_____
_____

54

A Christian should have a low self-esteem.

As we have already seen, the Bible tells us to love God first and our neighbors as ourselves. In Philippians 2:3, Paul admonishes to esteem others above ourselves.

To esteem is to respect and admire, or to consider. If we are to love and honor God first, respect and have consideration for our neighbors above ourselves, then where should self-esteem be?

Last. Therefore, a low self-esteem is a Christian's disposition.

But we must have a healthy *self-image*; an accurate understanding of our IDENTITY. Who are you?

Remember that acronym, JOY:

Jesus first,
Others next,
You last.

To esteem God means:

55

Don't allow your past to gag you.

That you did something wrong in the past is no reason for you not to advocate against it now that you are a child of God. The difference between then and now is the Blood of Jesus.

There is therefore now no condemnation to them which are in Christ Jesus, who walk not after the flesh, but after the Spirit (Romans 8:1).

Paul, who wrote these words under the inspiration of the Holy Spirit, consented to the death of Christianity's first martyr, Stephen, and caused such devastation among the Christians that they initially doubted his conversion. Yet, after his conversion, he spoke against zeal without knowledge and against murder.

Jesus conquered sin and death for you. If you have confessed your sins and turned to Him as both Lord and Savior, then do not fear. Open your mouth. Speak for Jesus. But remember His words: "Sin no more." (John 5:14, 8:11.)

Today, I have decided that by God's grace, I will no longer be silent about:

_____
_____
_____
_____
_____
_____
_____
_____
_____
_____
_____
_____
_____
_____
_____

56

No woman who is aware of her worth needs to walk up or down a street, waving a placard to remind everyone that she is a woman.

A real woman can be identified without her ever saying a word. She does not need to remind anyone that she is a woman. That ornament of a meek and quiet spirit, which is in the sight of God of great price (1 Peter 3:4), is the classic identifier of a confident, assured, God-fearing woman.

Bible verses that encourage me to be meek and quiet are:

_____
_____
_____
_____
_____
_____
_____
_____
_____
_____
_____
_____
_____
_____
_____

58

Some things require flight, not fasting or fellowship.

Do not waste your time contemplating or fasting about things for which the Bible has given you the simple and urgent commandment to flee. Run away!

Flee fornication. Every sin that a man doeth is without the body; but he that committeth fornication sinneth against his own body (1 Corinthians 6:18).

Wherefore, my dearly beloved, flee from idolatry (1 Corinthians 10:14).

But thou, O man of God, flee these things; and follow after righteousness, godliness, faith, love, patience, meekness (1 Timothy 6:11).

Flee also youthful lusts: but follow righteousness, faith, charity, peace, with them that call on the Lord out of a pure heart (2 Timothy 2:22).

Nobody is going to look for you and flee on your behalf. Place one foot in front of the other. Rinse and repeat at a very high speed.

With immediate effect, I need to let go of:

_____
_____
_____
_____
_____
_____
_____
_____
_____
_____
_____
_____
_____
_____
_____

59

A good wife must manage the little things.

By little and little

By little and little I will drive them out from before thee, until thou be increased, and inherit the land (Exodus 23:30).

The victory for some battles is not always manifested in one fell swoop.

God told the Israelites that He would drive out their enemies before them little by little, so that the land would not be left bare for animals to multiply and overwhelm them. In the same way, sometimes he deliberately wins battles for us little by little, so that we are not overwhelmed. With each step of victory, the child of God matures enough and gathers the experience and patience to handle the next step. Like John Gill explains, of this verse,

> As their enemies were driven out gradually, by little and little, so they multiplied gradually, until at length they became a sufficient number to fill all the cities and towns in all the nations of Canaan, and take an entire possession of it, as their inheritance given unto them by God.

Little foxes

Take us the foxes, the little foxes, that spoil the vines: for our vines have tender grapes (Song of Solomon 2:15).

Foxes are sly and cause destruction. With the exception of Jesus mentioning that they have dens, wherever they are seen in scripture, they are either causing or aiding destruction or used as a symbol of destruction and guile. (In fact, it is interesting that Jesus said that they, in all their character, had dens, but the Son of man had nowhere to lay His head. Isn't it interesting how the foolish prophets, who are like foxes in the deserts, are so well-received today, yet Jesus Himself is so rejected even within so-called churches?)

Here, they signify false teaching. Even the "smallest" of heresies must be exposed and destroyed, before it destroys the young converts.

Every woman will have to contend with foxes in her marriage. Whether it be the foxes of financial challenges, nagging, focus shifting from spouse to children, different cultures, in-laws, being critical, etc., every woman must immediately nip them in the bud. Because it is when little foxes are ignored that they grw into not just bigger foxes, but more foxes.

It is the woman that builds the home, per Proverbs 14. A wife must have the prudence, the sobriety, the discretion and the faith to ensure that no foxes gnaw and scratch at her marriage. This definitely cannot be done without God.

Little children.

Suffer little children, and forbid them not, to come unto me: for of such is the kingdom of heaven (Matthew 19:14).

Not only are we to have faith like little children; we are also not to dare to forbid – through our actions, words, or observed examples – these children to come to Jesus. It is better, Jesus told us, for a person to be thrown into the sea with a millstone tied around his neck than to cause a child to stumble (Luke 17:2).

Children, I have come to discover, do not learn as much from words as they do by imitation. Train up a child in the way he should go, and when he is old, he will not depart from it. You are training your children every time they look at or listen to you (Proverbs 22:6). God will hold all mothers accountable.

A little leaven

A little leaven leaveneth the whole lump. (1 Corinthians 5:6, Galatians 5:9).

Just a bit of yeast will make a mountain of dough rise. In the Bible, leaven is a symbol of sin. Just a sprinkle, and a whole group of people can be influenced. In marriage, small things can blow up and cause divorce.

The one thing that yeast needs is time. Dough can rise in as little as 45 minutes. But yeast, which is a fungus and therefore living, can be killed at several different stages during the cooking or baking stage.

One method is using hot water. If that does not work, salt often will.

Every woman must ensure that leaven does not *linger in* her life or her marriage. That snide comment in public, that eye-roll, that hiss may look very little, but unless it is resolved or repented of immediately, it will cause problems in the long run.

Tone of voice is something I hear often as a problem in communication between men and women. I personally am still working on it. But the Bible tells us that a soft answer turns away wrath (Proverbs 15:1). How interesting that it also tells us to season our words with salt, and not coat them with sugar (Colossians 4:6). Yeast thrives tremendously in sugar.

A little folly

Dead flies cause the ointment of the apothecary to send forth a stinking savour: so doth a little folly him that is in reputation for wisdom and honour (Ecclesiastes 10:1).

This is self-explanatory. Just one foolish mistake can cost a woman her reputation. It is imperative that we pray, like David did in the 16th and 19th Psalms:

Preserve me, O God: for in Thee do I put my trust. I have set the Lord always before me: because he is at my right hand, I shall not be moved. Let the words of my mouth, and the meditation of my heart, be acceptable in Thy sight, O Lord, my Strength, and my Redeemer.

Gathering little.

He that had gathered much had nothing over; and he that had gathered little had no lack (Exodus 16:18, 2 Corinthians 8:15.

When God provided manna for the Israelites in the wilderness as they journeyed towards Canaan, he did so with instructions. A specific amount was to be collected each day, with the exception of Fridays, when they would collect enough for both that day and the Sabbath, as the latter was a holy day on which nobody was supposed to work.

However, some of the people do not seem to have trusted that God would continually provide, so they gathered more on the first occasion than was instructed. The extra manna "bred worms and stank", defeating the purpose of gathering it in the first place (Exodus 16:20).

In the Lord's Prayer, Jesus taught us to say "Give us this day our daily bread." (Matthew 6:11.) He also commanded us not to worry, for each day comes with its own troubles (Matthew 6:34). It can be difficult to see where provision will come from when things seem difficult, but God who provided Himself a Lamb (Genesis 22:8) will not fail to provide your needs. It would do us well to trust Him, so that our efforts do not breed worms and stink.

Always be sure that you are contemplating needs, and not wants, lest you falsely assume that provision has been withheld.

Having food and raiment, let us therewith be content.

And having food and raiment let us be therewith content. But they that will be rich fall into temptation and a snare, and into many foolish and hurtful lusts, which drown men in destruction and perdition. For the love of money is the root of all evil: which while some coveted after, they have erred from the faith, and pierced themselves through with many sorrows. (1 Timothy 6:8-10.)

They that will be rich – in other words, they that desire to be rich, or those whose will or longing it is to be rich. Let money never find any love in your heart for it, for nobody can serve both God and mammon (Matthew 6:24).

A little sleep

Yet a little sleep, a little slumber, a little folding of the hands to sleep: So shall thy poverty come as one that travelleth; and thy want as an armed man (Proverbs 6:10-11, 24:33-34).

This verse is a simple call to awakeness, alertness, and diligence. The book of Proverbs has many harsh words to say about laziness. Remember that these verses also apply spiritually, and that the prayer of prevention is better than the prayer of cure. Let us not let our warm blankets lure us away from the battle.

Here a little, there a little.

For precept must be upon precept, precept upon precept; line upon line, line upon line; here a little, and there a little. (Isaiah 28:10.)

God deals with us step by step. As someone dear to me once said, you cannot ask God to take you to the nations if you have not fulfilled commands you may see as nondescript and take for granted because this generation looks down on them, such as honoring parents. Your first ministry, as a wife, is to your husband.

It does not matter if you are Prophetess Jane Kalekye Musau of the Dunamis Hosanna Metanoia Talitha International Ministries. If you are married to John Mbugua, heaven knows you as Jane Mbugua. John knows you as Jane Mbugua. Stick all the titles and medals you want on yourself if you want, but please submit with them on. Welcome your husband home with them on. Serve your husband with them on. Your body is your husband's with them on. Even if he watches you on TV at 6pm, when you get home at 7, remember to go and cut those onions and begin to prepare his supper.

While I am on that point, please allow me to point out that the Bible says that when a man leaves his father and mother and cleaves to his wife, the two shall become one flesh (Genesis 2:24, Matthew 19:5, Mark 10:8, Ephesians 5:31). Kalekye, do not hold on to your father's name or try to hyphenate your name simply to sound modern. You have left Mr. Musau's home.

If you want to remain Jane Musau, please remember to include your name separately each time you pray for the Mbuguas, because you have refused to become a Mbugua. If you ask God to bless the

Mbugua dynasty, whose name you have refused to take on, will that prayer include you in it?

Be sure not to let fashion derail you from favor. If two are one flesh, my personal view is that they should have one name.

Honor your husband. Respect him. We were given Sarah as an example. So if, like Abraham, he is told to get up and go to a place where God will show him, please pack all your International and Dunamis and follow your husband to that place that God will show him.

Faithful in least, faithful in much.

He that is faithful in that which is least is faithful also in much: and he that is unjust in the least is unjust also in much. (Luke 16:10.)

Sometimes, it may appear that certain things can change if one big thing happens.

A single woman might think, "Oh, if only I were married! Then I would be happy."

But a married woman might think, "If only I were single! Then I would pursue this ministry."

A church member might think "If only I had a million! Then I would give thousands."

The millionaire might think, "If only these pastors were trustworthy! I would spare even my last penny."

A receptionist might think, "If only I were a manager! Then I would be nice to customers."

The CEO might think, "If only I had not made the mistakes I made as a receptionist! Then they would listen to what I have to say about customer service."

A businesswoman might think, "If only I had more capital! Then I would really get something good started."

Her competitor might think, "If only I had more time! Then I would really get this good thing going."

Moses may as well have said, "If only I were a good orator! Then I would be courageous enough."

The man at the pool may as well have said, "If only I had a man! Then I might have left here 37 years ago."

A wife might be saying, "If only I had married so-and-so! Then I would not be stuck in this submission misery."

Or,

"If only God had given me a sensible husband! Then I would truly, truly submit."

But while Moses was giving excuses at Horeb (Exodus 4), God asked him, "What do you have in your hand?"

That rod Moses held was used several times during the exodus of the Israelites from Egypt.

What do you have in your hand?

Choose joy within your singleness, for joy does not automatically descend on brides on the wedding day.

Choose joy within your marriage, for your single days are gone, and God can still use you - and still enable you to carry out that ministry.

Give out of your tens, whether minutes or dollars, and see God give back to you as men pour into your bosom, good measure, pressed down, shaken together, running over (Luke 6:38).

Be nice to customers, for one might see your kindness and ask your boss, "Whose damsel is this?" (Ruth 2:5.) Ruth was elevated higher than the servants that left grain for her to glean.

Forget the past, dear CEO, and speak anyway; do not let your past gag you (Philippians 3:13-14).

Get something good started with what you have in your hand. God will guide you.

Use your time wisely, and do your best to keep the good thing going.

Submit anyway, dear wife, and watch your marriage flourish.

Wisdom is what it takes.

Wisdom is the principal thing; therefore get wisdom: and with all thy getting get understanding (Proverbs 4:7).

If any of you lack wisdom, let him ask of God, that giveth to all men liberally, and upbraideth not; and it shall be given him. But let him ask in faith, nothing wavering. For he that wavereth is like a wave of the sea driven with the wind and tossed. For let not that man think that he shall receive any thing of the Lord. (James 1:5-7).

A little while.

It is a blessing that God created times and seasons. Can you imagine what life would be like if everything was permanent?

There are two things I think every woman must remember, regarding a *little while*:

Firstly, that wickedness is not permanent. Do not allow evil to cause you to fret. Abide in Jesus.

For yet a little while, and the wicked shall not be: yea, thou shalt diligently consider his place, and it shall not be (Psalm 37:10).

Secondly, we are living in the last days.

For yet a little while, and he that shall come will come, and will not tarry. (Hebrews 10:37).

Let us remain alert, live righteously, and keep our eyes on Jesus.

God, give me wisdom…:

60

Pray the "expose" prayer.

Many times throughout scripture, God tells us to call to Him, pray to Him, ask Him, seek Him.

In any situation where you are not clear on a person's intentions, simply ask God to reveal who this person is. Go to Him genuinely, and ask Him to expose their intentions.

Whether it is a person you want to vote for or a man who has asked to marry you; whether it is a potential client or supplier or a person giving a prophecy, do not feel the need to rush to do or accept anything without consulting God.

Even prophets sometimes get it wrong. Remember Samuel getting ready to anoint a son of Jesse as commanded by God? Had he gone with his feelings, he would have anointed the wrong son. Over and over, God said, "No. This is not him."

"Look not on his countenance," God told Samuel, "or on the height of his stature; because I have refused him: for the Lord seeth not as man seeth; for man looketh on the outward appearance, but the Lord looketh on the heart."

It is that heart that you may need the Lord to reveal to you from time to time when making difficult or crucial decisions.

Remember that one-second "No" or "Go"? Listen for it. Obey Him. The prayer of prevention is better than the prayer of cure.

61

The woman who feeds her man keeps her man.

I have come to realize that men are very simple creatures. All a man needs from his wife is **to be fed**. I might have the order wrong, but if you want to keep your husband happy, "feed" (fill) his stomach, feed his spirit, feed his ego, feed his sex drive.

While we see men, including Jesus Himself, cooking in the Bible, Proverbs 31:15 says the virtuous woman rises at dawn to prepare food for her family as well as her servants.

You might also say, "But what does he get to do?" That is why it is good to ask whether you are in it to have a husband or to be a wife.

"But I do my part! He is the one at fault!" To whom are you ultimately answerable; him or God? Be careful about this attitude, because marriage, as has been said, is two forgivers living together, and, more importantly, on the day that you give account before God, it will be for you and your life – alone – that you will give account.

Regarding feeding his spirit, a virtuous woman is an encourager. She does her best not to tear her husband down. She affirms him and appreciates him. While these things might not make much sense to women, I have come to learn that "respect" is so much more than saying "I respect you". While many women feel the need to hear "I love you", men, from what they tell me, would rather see and experience respect than hear it. He would rather feel respected than hear that he is respected.

When I say "feed his ego", I do not mean flatter the man and focus on puffing him up. I mean remind him, from time to time, of some of the reasons why you appreciate him, and, beyond the words, respect him both in private and in public.

Consider Abigail, in 1 Samuel 25. David was on his way to kill her entire household when she hurriedly decided to meet and plead with him.

Abigail... fell before David on her face, and bowed herself to the ground, and fell at his feet, and said... the Lord will certainly make my lord a sure house; because my lord fighteth the battles of the Lord, and evil hath not been found in thee all thy days...

The soul of my lord shall be bound in the bundle of life with the Lord thy God; and the souls of thine enemies, them shall he sling out, as out of the middle of a sling.

And it shall come to pass, when the Lord shall have done to my lord according to all the good that he hath spoken concerning thee, and shall have appointed thee ruler over Israel;

That this shall be no grief unto thee, nor offence of heart unto my lord, either that thou hast shed blood causeless, or that my lord hath avenged himself: but when the Lord shall have dealt well with my lord, then remember thine handmaid.

(1 Samuel 25:23-31.)

Abigail, knowing David was angry, quickly alighted and bowed before him in respect. Throughout her speech, she referred to him as "my lord". She reminded him that he was a man of God – "my lord fighteth the battles of the Lord", and told him evil had not been found in him, perhaps implying that he might ruin this record if he killed her husband. She encouraged him not to shed blood, reminding him that God was with him. By mentioning the sling, she seems to have used tact to remind him of his victory over Goliath. She pleaded that be not forget her when he became king, as she was sure he would be.

Abigail became David's wife a very short while later, after the death of her husband.

As for the sex drive, the Bible is clear.

The wife hath not power of her own body, but the husband: and likewise also the husband hath not power of his own body, but the wife. (1 Corinthians 7:4.)

Do not poison your husband. Do not starve him. Nourish him. May God strengthen us all.

Fifteen good wives in the Bible, from whose example I can learn, are:

_____
_____
_____
_____
_____
_____
_____
_____
_____
_____
_____
_____
_____
_____
_____

62

Know your price.

Every woman needs to know her price. It is very easy for a woman who does not know her price to be sold out to anyone or anything.

Disagree? Allow me to refer you to Genesis 3.

God has placed in every woman the power to influence not only men, but also nations and generations.

In this day and age, where Christ has redeemed us from the curse of the law and we are seated in heavenly places in Him (Ephesians 2:6), it is an abomination for any woman to let anything good die or stay dead on her watch.

Every woman is a bearer – a life-bearer, fruit-bearer, flag-bearer, torch-bearer, burden-bearer, image-bearer, office-bearer, bearer of grace and truth.

Every woman is an influencer with no excuse. "Influencer" is not a job title, nor does it belong to people on YouTube or in titled positions.

Like Rahab pleaded in Joshua 2 for her family members' lives, the woman must plead for the salvation of those around her.

Like Esther, she knows that she has been created for such a time as this and will risk her life approaching kings so that her people are not extinguished. She is ready to rally women to fast where the need may arise (Esther 4:16).

Like the Shunammite in 2 Kings 4, she secures blessings for the next generation and receives a prophet's reward (Matthew 10:41-42) because she recognizes prophets in her midst and honors them.

Like Bathsheba who secured the kingdom for her son, she thinks ahead and remembers God's promises and the king's words to her.

I'm reminded of a woman named Jehoshabeath who hid the king's son from his wicked grandmother, and in so doing secured his place as the royal heir (2 Chronicles 22:11).

Everywhere a good woman is found, she is *securing* something great not for herself, but for others.

Finally, remember Paul's words in 1 Corinthians 6:20 and 7:23: *For ye are bought with a price: therefore glorify God in your body, and in your spirit, which are God's.*

63

A woman who twists her mouth will twist her home.

For some reason, women seem to have this strange power to hold on to things that offend them. Because they cannot contest the Bible's admonition to submit, many times women try to control things in other ways – using their bodies or sulking, for example.

What I am about to say is not the only, or even the main reason why this manipulation should be shunned. But while you are busy trying to win a fight, your maid is busy serving your husband's food with a curtsey; the secretary is busy serving coffee with a smile; the messenger says, "Yes, sir. No, sir." They are determined to win the man. Some maids are deliberately sent to homes with the instruction to remember where they came from. "Go and get a promotion," some mothers say to their daughters. "He is a good and rich man. Elevate your family's social class."

While you're ignoring your boyfriend's texts, fake friends may be saying "no rings attached, no strings attached", providing the emotional support he is looking for as you reject him, and subtly planting seeds of doubt in his mind, presenting themselves as model potential wives. I'm not saying live a paranoid life. I'm saying know that you are not the only one who knows and sees what you have.

Remember, wives, and let me spell it out again:

If in your house there exists a treasure known as "husband", guard this treasure jealously. Most know its worth. Many pray and fast for it. Many devise schemes to steal it. Some don't think you deserve it, yet God gave it to YOU.

Is that month-long silence, coupled with nightly balancing on the edge of your bed, really worth it?

64

A woman who refuses to be humble will be humbled.

The Bible says God resists the proud, but gives grace to the humble (James 4:6). To resist a person is to meet everything they do with an equal or greater force than they have applied. And to be resisted by God Himself is to be in the worst of all possible states.

God resists the proud. In other words, the God of the universe sets Himself against anybody who is proud. He does not send any angel – He personally sees to it that this person's plans are frustrated. The Bible tells us that if God be for us, nobody can be against us (Romans 8:31). Amen to that; but where will a person go if God Himself is against him/her? Pride, you see, is the quickest route to destruction.

Humility (being humble) is so much better and so much easier than humiliation (being humbled).

Fifteen examples of humility in the Bible are:

_____
_____
_____
_____
_____
_____
_____
_____
_____
_____
_____
_____
_____
_____
_____

65

Pitch a tent.

In all things, the Lord is speaking. If you find yourself in a situation where you have had a disagreement with someone, or are not happy about a situation at work, or are grieving unrequited love, do metaphorically what Abraham did a number of times in actuality: pitch a "tent" where you are and build an altar to God. In other words, take a moment to seek God seriously and vulnerably about this issue. Ask, "Lord, what does this say about my relationship with You?" Because that is always, always what it is about.

Seek Him in His Word. As He speaks to you, listen. As He gives instructions, obey. Cling to Jesus, and Jesus only, for your healing.

God, please show me what Your will is in this situation and speak to me about:

_____
_____
_____
_____
_____
_____
_____
_____
_____
_____
_____
_____
_____
_____

66

God knows all, sees all, rewards all and avenges all.

He knows all – from your greatest triumphs to your deepest struggles. He created time, and therefore it is wise to obey Him, as He knows the dangers that may lie ahead, no matter how good things look, or the joys that may lie ahead, no matter how dire things look. 1 John 3:20 is clear on His omniscience.

He sees all – Nothing escapes the eyes of the God who never sleeps nor slumbers (Psalm 121). That means if we represent Him, He sees us. In our private moments, He sees us. *All things are naked and opened unto the eyes of Him with whom we have to do* (Hebrews 4:13).

He rewards all – He gives to all their just desserts. People may not see what you have gone through in yielding to Him and taking the steps He commands you to in this walk with Him, but He does, and He will reward you.

And let us not be weary in well doing, for in due time, you will reap, if you faint not (Galatians 6:9).

He avenges all – Refuse to agree to take matters into your own hands. I type this knowing how difficult that is to do, but exhorting you – and myself: vengeance is God's alone. He reminds us of this in Deuteronomy 32:35 and in Romans 12:17-19. Let us be still. He will fight for us.

67

Not all "gospel" is The Gospel.

I. The Gospel is not a "hustle". It is not a job, a 9-5, a main gig, a side gig or any other gig. It is the good news that because of Jesus Christ, man can have eternal life.

II. It is not an "industry", or a fun thing people do in their extra time so that they can make money or be given awards by other people based on standards human standards that blatantly exclude God.

III. Not everyone who does or sings "gospel" is sent by God, because not all gospels are the Gospel.

IV. Not everything titled "Christian" these days is of Christ.

V. Wake up.

To sing and pray with my spirit and with my understanding (1 Corinthians 14:15) means:

_____
_____
_____
_____
_____
_____
_____
_____
_____
_____
_____
_____
_____
_____

68

If you will not correct me, I don't want your friendship.

A true friend will never cheer one on as one cruises speedily towards the edge of a cliff. Anyone who is afraid to tell a friend the truth has placed his or her fear of the friend's reaction above the friend's eternal destination and current walk with God.

Is that friendship? Not the real or true kind, for sure!

As a friend, I should:

_____
_____
_____
_____
_____
_____
_____
_____
_____
_____
_____
_____
_____
_____
_____
_____

69

If you do not obey one, how will you be entrusted with two?

Sometimes, God instructs us to do things that may appear inconsequential, or that are done differently from the way we would do them. Acts 8 is one of many passages that demonstrate the importance of obedience.

Philip was once minding his business when God told him "Arise, and go toward the south unto the way that goeth down from Jerusalem unto Gaza, which is desert."

The Bible says that Philip simply "arose and went." Many today would first check emails, maybe even bank accounts; make a few phone calls; set up a vacation response; have lunch, grab an extra set of clothes, just in case...

Philip simply "arose and went: and, behold, a man of Ethiopia, an eunuch of great authority under Candace queen of the Ethiopians, who had the charge of all her treasure... had come to Jerusalem for to worship."

The Lord told Philip to go near, and join himself to the chariot. He obeyed again, and struck a conversation with this man that ended with the man becoming born again and being baptized.

See the beauty of God's timing, and the importance of obedience. Had Philip taken his time, would he have encountered the chariot at that exact spot, with the eunuch reading what we now know as Isaiah 53? Would they have gotten to the body of water at the exact time that they did?

The apostle Peter had a similar experience, as we see in Acts 12. The Bible says that he was in jail, and that from the time he had been arrested, the church had not ceased to pray for him. God answered - even sooner than they thought, as is evident in 12:15, but back to prison:

Fast asleep, Peter is struck on the side by an angel. "Arise up quickly," he is instructed. His chains fall off his hands.

The angel says, "Get dressed and put on your sandals," which he does. Finally, he is told, "Put on your coat and follow me."

Imagine if the angel had said, "Quick! Get up!" and Peter had asked for five more minutes of sleep.

Imagine if he had been told, "Get up!" and he had instead tried to put on his shoes. Would he have been able to? No; he was still chained.

Imagine if he had been ordered "Follow me!" and he decided to dictate the route or suggest a short-cut, or, even, said "I know my way around, I'll be fine."

Obedience in even what may appear to be the simplest of matters is crucial. And if we do not fulfill the first step obediently, we will probably not be able to move to the next.

God, forgive me for not being obedient when:

_____
_____
_____
_____
_____
_____
_____
_____
_____
_____
_____
_____
_____
_____
_____
_____

70

You have One Relevant Audience.

When you wake up in the morning and put on that make up, who are you doing it for? Who did you have in mind when you decided to get that degree, buy those shoes, get that tattoo, go vegetarian, get married?

Why do you walk around with that bottled water and go to the gym? Why are you on that diet? Why do you want to gain or lose weight? Why do you like that song so much? Why do you have that job? Or why are you looking for that other job?

If no human being would ever find out that you drive that Range Rover, went to a particular place, stayed at a particular hotel, would you have bought it, gone there, stayed there?

In short, who are you trying to impress? Whose approval are you seeking? From whom do you derive your significance?

What do you do when you think nobody is looking? That, my dear, is your character. Guess what - God knows it. Just when you think you're all alone, there's always someone watching. He sees every single word and action, but not just that; He sees every thought as well. He sees what you harbor in the parts of you that no man can see. He sees those things about you that even you cannot see: the jealousy at a friend's success; the lies you tell yourself; the things you think you can't do; the in-ward sneer at that unbeliever; the fears and frustrations; the selfish tears bred by covetousness; the dirty movie scenes you watch without a flinch.

God sees everything, as we have already been reminded. He alone matters, because it is to Him that we answer and will answer. Let this truth bring both comfort and sobriety as you close this book and head out to do what He called you to do.

The eyes of the LORD are in every place, beholding the evil and the good. (Proverbs 15.3.)

Be abundantly blessed! May the grace of our Lord Jesus Christ, and the love of God, and the fellowship of the Holy Spirit, be with you and yours now and forever, Amen.

God Loves You!

He created you to be in perfect relationship with Him. Sadly, sin fractures that relationship and separates people from Him. We can only be forgiven and reconciled back to God through His Son, Jesus Christ.

1. YOUR CHEQUE

The loving God created us to be in a perfect relationship with Him. He created a perfect world, and then created human beings to live in it. There was no evil at all – no sin, sorrow, death, fear, shame, or guilt – in the world at that time. God also gave man free will. Sadly, the first man that was created, Adam, used this free will to disobey God. It was at that moment that sin came into the world, and separated us from God. Because we all come from Adam, we inherited his sin, in almost the same way as we inherit our ethnicities from our biological parents.

God is Just, and will therefore not rip us off. He will give us just wages. We reap what we sow. Just like the salary for your job is a cheque, the salary, or wages, of sin is death. Just like you expect and deserve a cheque after a 40-hour workweek or at the end of the month, after a life of sin, a human being deserves death. Good deeds don't change that. The holiest standard to man, and the greatest "good deeds", are as dirty as used tampons to God, because in addition to being loving and just, God is holy. In our own strength, we *cannot* obey God's law. We each, we all, fall short. The Bible, which can be described as a letter from God to us, says that, and also tells us that those who sin will go to a real place full of torment known as hell. That means every single descendant of Adam deserves hell.

2. YOUR GIFT

God is Just, but He is also Love, and He doesn't want us to die (remember, He created us to be with and worship Him). So He sent His only begotten Son (you know John 3:16? It's actually true!), also referred to as the Last Adam, to die in our place, receive our wages for us, and give us a free gift instead - eternal life. Jesus is the only Son of God that is *begotten* – the only one who is directly fathered by God, and this happened so that we could freely become *adopted* children of God.

As you know, a gift is free only to the receiver. Someone has to pay for it. Jesus paid for your gift with His Blood. Because He was a perfect Man, He could die for other men. He rose from the dead three days after He was brutally murdered on a cross in a process that included betrayal, public mockery, and abuse. Scientists have proven his death to have been extremely physically and emotionally painful. Words like "ex***cruci****ating*" have their root in the kind of pain experienced during ***cruci***fixion. Still, Jesus rose again, proving that death had no power over Him. Hundreds saw Him then; many still see Him today. His death and resurrection secured your gift. Eternal life is available for YOU. Despite our sin, there is a way to be reconciled to God; to be restored to that original relationship He wants with us. But we all know that a package at your door or a gift under a tree with your name on it only helps you if you pick it up, open it, receive it rather than reject it, and use it. This good news – the announcement that you can be restored to God and that He still loves you - is called the Gospel.

3. YOUR CHOICE

The simple way to receive your free gift is simply to receive and begin to walk with Jesus. That simply means putting your total trust in Him alone – not your friends, parents, pastor, husband, not any other human being; not even yourself. The scriptures (God's letter to us) tell us that all you need to do is

(a) admit your need for God and the fact that you are responsible for excluding Him from your life and disobeying His law;
(b) open your mouth and say 'Jesus Christ is Lord';

(c) Believe in your heart that He is, and that God raised Him from the dead.

It's that simple. From that moment, eternal life begins. Freedom begins.

4. YOUR MOVE

Ready to receive this gift? Say a short prayer, in your own words. It could be something like this:

"Father in heaven, I confess that I am a sinner. I've lived my life for me. I realize that none of my works and achievements can ever get me into heaven. I'm sorry for my sins and for the life I've lived. Please forgive me. I want a new beginning with You. With all my heart, I believe Jesus died in my place and is alive. From this moment on, I choose to trust Him alone. Jesus, You're alive, so I know You can hear me. You are not only Lord, but *my* Lord. Fill me with Your Holy Spirit. Help me to obey You and do Your will every day. Lead me to people who walk with You, and teach me how to pray and how to read Your Word. Thank You for saving me. In Jesus' Name, Amen."

Ask God to lead you to a church that teaches what the scriptures say. That will help you grow in Him and develop that relationship He longs to have with you.

5 A PARTY FOR YOU!

If you said the prayer above, then angels are celebrating because you just made the most important decision of your life. I celebrate with you!

"I tell you that in the same way there will be more rejoicing in heaven over one sinner who repents than over ninety- nine righteous persons who do not need to repent." ~ Luke 15:7

SCRIPTURE REFERENCES: Deuteronomy 32:4, Isaiah 64:6, John 3:16, Romans 3:23, Romans 6:23, Romans 10:9, Galatians 6:7, 1 John 4:15

ABOUT THE AUTHOR
Paula is a servant of God, loved, called, chosen, and helped by Jesus Christ.

www.ingramcontent.com/pod-product-compliance
Lightning Source LLC
Chambersburg PA
CBHW051649040426
42446CB00009B/1055

57

It what it is because it has been allowed to be what it has become.

"It is what it is" is a common statement nowadays. Examined closely, it exposes itself as having within it a spirit of resignation, complacency, mediocrity, and even sheer laziness.

"It is what it is" is a statement made by a woman who does not feel like changing anything either by prayer or by action. A woman who has allowed pain to make her indifferent, feels no empathy or sympathy for others, even when she is the cause of their misery, and is convinced that things cannot change, will not feel the desire to make a difference or see the urgency of her much-needed contributions to her home, her colleagues, her clients, or the Body of Christ.

If you hate your mother-in-law and think it is what it is, wake up. Hate is no disposition for a Christian.

If you hear that your husband is having another affair and have decided it is what it is, wake up. No angel will come and fight for a marriage for which you have refused to fight yourself.

If your husband keeps calling you out on something, and you do not bat an eyelid as you tell him it is what it is, wake up. That is disrespect, and not only is it the type of marital sin that hinders prayers, there are also very many women around him willing to give him the respect you think only you can give.

If your children are crying out for attention but you unfeelingly decide you're busy and it is what it is, you need to snap out of it. No job is more important than the job of motherhood.

Wake up! Snap out of it! Open your eyes and leave that foggy laziness! Because if things actually become what you are tempting them to become, you might have more to deal with than you could have imagined, and the only person you will have to blame is yourself.

Do something. Say a prayer and trust God for the impossible. Make an effort. Extend mercy. Don't dismiss or give up on things so easily. Things may not really be what they appear to be, and the discernment and understanding you need can only come from God.